PUBLISHING

EXCITING

G000147143

THIS EXAM KIT COMES WITH
FREE ONLINE ACCESS
TO EXTRA RESOURCES AIMED AT HELPING YOU PASS YOUR EXAMS

IN ADDITION TO THE OFFICIAL QUESTIONS AND ANSWERS IN THIS BOOK, GO ONLINE AND EN-gage WITH:

- An iPaper version of the Exam Kit
- Articles including Key Examinable Areas
- Material updates
- Latest Official ACCA exam questions
- Extra question assistance using the Signpost icon
- Timed Questions with an online tutor debrief using the Clock icon

And you can access all of these extra resources anytime, anywhere using your EN-gage account.

How to access your online resources

If you are a Kaplan Financial tuition, full-time or distance learning student

You will already have an EN-gage account and these extra resources will be available to you online. You do not need to register again, as this process was completed when you enrolled. If having problems accessing online materials, please ask your course administrator.

If you purchased through Kaplan Flexible Learning or via the Kaplan Publishing website

You will automatically receive an e-mail invitation to EN-gage online. Please register your details using this e-mail to gain access to your content. If you do not receive the e-mail or book content, please contact our Technical Support team at engage@twinsystems.com.

If you are already a registered EN-gage user

Go to www.EN-gage.co.uk and log in. Select the 'add a book' feature and enter the ISBN number of this book and the unique pass key at the bottom of this card. Then click 'finished' or 'add another book'. You may add as many books as you have purchased from this screen.

If you are a new EN-gage user

Register at www.EN-gage.co.uk and click on the link contained in the e-mail we sent you to activate your account. Then select the 'add a book' feature, enter the ISBN number of this book and the unique pass key at the bottom of this card. Then click 'finished' or 'add another book'.

Your Code and Information

This code can only be used once for the registration of one book online. This registration will expire when the final sittings for the examinations covered by this book have taken place. Please allow one hour from the time you submitted your book details for us to process your request.

Please scratch the film to access your Engage code

Please be aware that this code is case-sensitive and you will need to include the dashes within the passcode, but not when entering the ISBN. For further technical support, please visit www.EN-gage.co.uk

ACCA

Paper F2

FIA

Diploma in Accounting and Business

Management Accounting (MA/FMA)

EXAM KIT

British Library Cataloguing-in-Publication Data

A catalogue record for this book is available from the British Library.

Published by:

Kaplan Publishing UK

Unit 2 The Business Centre

Molly Millar's Lane

Wokingham

Berkshire

RG41 2QZ

ISBN: 978-0-85732-309-5

© Kaplan Financial Limited, 2011

Printed in the UK by CPI William Clowes Beccles NR34 7TL

Acknowledgements

The past ACCA examination questions are the copyright of the Association of Chartered Certified Accountants. The original answers to the questions from June 1994 onwards were produced by the examiners themselves and have been adapted by Kaplan Publishing.

We are grateful to the Chartered Institute of Management Accountants and the Institute of Chartered Accountants in England and Wales for permission to reproduce past examination questions. The answers have been prepared by Kaplan Publishing.

CONTENTS

Section

New features in this edition

In addition to providing a wide ranging bank of practice questions, we have also included in this edition:

• Paper specific information and advice on exam technique.

• Our recommended approach to make your revision for this particular subject as effective as possible.

  This includes step by step guidance on how best to use our Kaplan material (Complete text, pocket notes and exam kit) at this stage in your studies.

You will find a wealth of other resources to help you with your studies on the following sites:

www.EN-gage.co.uk and www.accaglobal.com/students/

INDEX TO QUESTIONS AND ANSWERS

PRACTICE QUESTIONS

EXAM TECHNIQUE

- **Do not skip any of the material** in the syllabus.
- **Read each question** *very* carefully.
- **Double-check your answer** before committing yourself to it.
- Answer **every** question – if you do not know an answer, you don't lose anything by guessing. Think carefully before you **guess**. The examiner has indicated that many candidates are still leaving blank answers in the real exam.
- If you are answering a multiple-choice question, **eliminate first those answers that you know are wrong**. Then choose the most appropriate answer from those that are left.
- Remember that **only one answer to a multiple-choice question can be right**. After you have eliminated the ones that you know to be wrong, if you are still unsure, guess. Only guess after you have double-checked that you have only eliminated answers that are *definitely* wrong.
- **Don't panic** if you realise you've answered a question incorrectly. Getting one question wrong will not mean the difference between passing and failing

Computer-based exams – tips

- Do not attempt a CBE until you have **completed all study material** relating to it.
- On the ACCA website there is a CBE demonstration. It is **ESSENTIAL** that you attempt this before your real CBE. You will become familiar with how to move around the CBE screens and the way that questions are formatted, increasing your confidence and speed in the actual exam.
- Be sure you understand how to use the **software** before you start the exam. If in doubt, ask the assessment centre staff to explain it to you.
- Questions are **displayed on the screen** and answers are entered using keyboard and mouse. At the end of the exam, you are given a certificate showing the result you have achieved.
- In addition to the traditional multiple-choice question type, CBEs might also contain **other types of questions**, such as number entry questions, formula entry questions, and stem questions with multiple parts. There are also questions that carry several marks.
- You need to be sure you **know how to answer questions** of this type before you sit the exam, through practice.

KAPLAN PUBLISHING

PAPER SPECIFIC INFORMATION

THE EXAM

FORMAT OF THE PAPER-BASED AND COMPUTER BASED EXAM

Number of marks

50 compulsory multiple choice questions (2 marks each)   100

Total time allowed: 2 hours

Two mark questions will usually require you to make calculations in order to ascertain the correct answer and will comprise of the following answer types:

(i)   Multiple choice with four options (A, B, C or D)

(ii)   Require you to enter a numerical answer (CBE only)

(iii)   Ask you to select two correct answers from a choice of four

AIM

To develop knowledge and understanding of providing basic management information in an organisation to support management in planning and decision-making

OBJECTIVES

On successful completion of this paper, candidates should be able to:

*   explain the nature, source and purpose of management information

*   explain and apply cost accounting techniques

*   prepare budgets for planning and control

*   compare actual costs with standard costs and analyse any variances

*   analyse, interpret and monitor business performance

*   Two mark questions will usually comprise the following answer types:

    (i)   Multiple choice with four options (A, B, C or D)

    (ii)   Require you to enter a numerical answer (CBE only)

    (iii)   Ask you to select two correct answers from a choice of four

*   ACCA official statistics have shown that most students do not find the exam time pressured

PASS MARK

The pass mark for all ACCA Qualification examination papers is 50%.

DETAILED SYLLABUS

The detailed syllabus and study guide written by the ACCA can be found at:

www.**acca**global.com/students/

KAPLAN'S RECOMMENDED REVISION APPROACH

QUESTION PRACTICE IS THE KEY TO SUCCESS

Success in professional examinations relies upon you acquiring a firm grasp of the required knowledge at the tuition phase. In order to be able to do the questions, knowledge is essential.

However, the difference between success and failure often hinges on your exam technique on the day and making the most of the revision phase of your studies.

The **Kaplan complete text** is the starting point, designed to provide the underpinning knowledge to tackle all questions. However, in the revision phase, pouring over text books is not the answer.

Kaplan Online fixed tests help you consolidate your knowledge and understanding and are a useful tool to check whether you can remember key topic areas.

Kaplan pocket notes are designed to help you quickly revise a topic area, however you then need to practice questions. There is a need to progress to full exam standard questions as soon as possible, and to tie your exam technique and technical knowledge together.

The importance of question practice cannot be over-emphasised.

The recommended approach below is designed by expert tutors in the field, in conjunction with their knowledge of the examiner.

The approach taken for the fundamental papers is to revise by topic area.

You need to practice as many questions as possible in the time you have left.

OUR AIM

Our aim is to get you to the stage where you can attempt exam standard questions confidently, to time, in a closed book environment, with no supplementary help (i.e. to simulate the real examination experience).

Practising your exam technique on real past examination questions, in timed conditions, is also vitally important for you to assess your progress and identify areas of weakness that may need more attention in the final run up to the examination.

The approach below shows you which questions you should use to build up to coping with exam standard question practice, and references to the sources of information available should you need to revisit a topic area in more detail.

Remember that in the real examination, all you have to do is:

- attempt all questions required by the exam
- only spend the allotted time on each question, and
- get them at least 50% right!

Try and practice this approach on every question you attempt from now to the real exam.

THE KAPLAN PAPER F2 REVISION PLAN

Stage 1: Assess areas of strengths and weaknesses

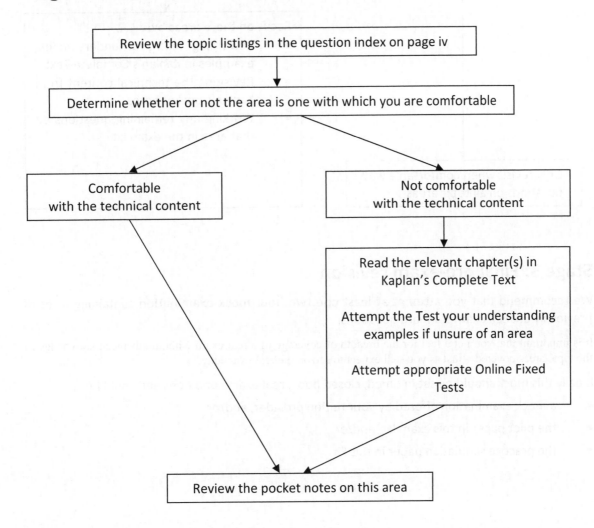

Review the topic listings in the question index on page iv

Determine whether or not the area is one with which you are comfortable

Comfortable with the technical content

Not comfortable with the technical content

Read the relevant chapter(s) in Kaplan's Complete Text

Attempt the Test your understanding examples if unsure of an area

Attempt appropriate Online Fixed Tests

Review the pocket notes on this area

Stage 2: Practice questions

Ensure that you revise all syllabus areas as questions could be asked on anything.

Try to avoid referring to text books and notes and the model answer until you have completed your attempt.

Try to answer the question in the allotted time.

Review your attempt with the model answer. If you got the answer wrong, can you see why? Was the problem a lack of knowledge or a failure to understand the question fully?

Fill in the self-assessment box below and decide on your best course of action.

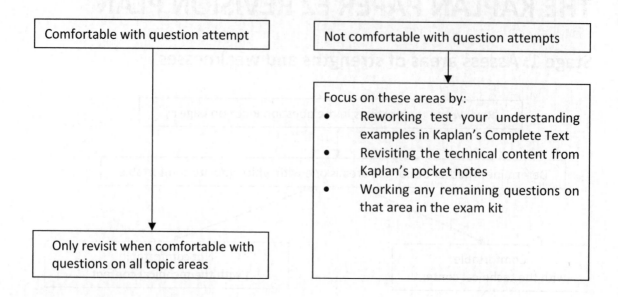

Stage 3: Final pre-exam revision

We recommend that you **attempt at least one two hour mock examination** containing a set of previously unseen exam standard questions.

It is important that you get a feel for the breadth of coverage of a real exam without advanced knowledge of the topic areas covered – just as you will expect to see on the real exam day.

Ideally this mock should be sat in timed, closed book, real exam conditions and could be:

- a mock examination offered by your tuition provider, and/or

- the pilot paper in this exam kit, and/or

- the practice simulation paper in this kit

FORMULAE AND TABLES

Regression analysis

$y = a + bx$

$$a = \frac{\sum y}{n} - \frac{b \sum x}{n}$$

$$b = \frac{n \sum xy - \sum x \sum y}{n \sum x^2 - (\sum x)^2}$$

$$r = \frac{n \sum xy - \sum x \sum y}{\sqrt{\left(n \sum x^2 - (\sum x)^2\right)\left(n \sum y^2 - (\sum y)^2\right)}}$$

Economic order quantity

$$= \sqrt{\frac{2C_0 D}{C_h}}$$

Economic batch quantity

$$= \sqrt{\frac{2C_0 D}{C_h \left(1 - \dfrac{D}{R}\right)}}$$

KAPLAN PUBLISHING

PRESENT VALUE TABLE

Present value of 1, i.e. $(1 + r)^{-n}$

Where r = interest rate

        n = number of periods until payment.

Periods (n)	Discount rate (r) 1%	2%	3%	4%	5%	6%	7%	8%	9%	10%
1	0.990	0.980	0.971	0.962	0.952	0.943	0.935	0.926	0.917	0.909
2	0.980	0.961	0.943	0.925	0.907	0.890	0.873	0.857	0.842	0.826
3	0.971	0.942	0.915	0.889	0.864	0.840	0.816	0.794	0.772	0.751
4	0.961	0.924	0.888	0.855	0.823	0.792	0.763	0.735	0.708	0.683
5	0.951	0.906	0.863	0.822	0.784	0.747	0.713	0.681	0.650	0.621
6	0.942	0.888	0.837	0.790	0.746	0.705	0.666	0.630	0.596	0.564
7	0.933	0.871	0.813	0.760	0.711	0.665	0.623	0.583	0.547	0.513
8	0.923	0.853	0.789	0.731	0.677	0.627	0.582	0.540	0.502	0.467
9	0.914	0.837	0.766	0.703	0.645	0.592	0.544	0.500	0.460	0.424
10	0.905	0.820	0.744	0.676	0.614	0.558	0.508	0.463	0.422	0.386
11	0.896	0.804	0.722	0.650	0.585	0.527	0.475	0.429	0.388	0.350
12	0.887	0.788	0.701	0.625	0.557	0.497	0.444	0.397	0.356	0.319
13	0.879	0.773	0.681	0.601	0.530	0.469	0.415	0.368	0.326	0.290
14	0.870	0.758	0.661	0.577	0.505	0.442	0.388	0.340	0.299	0.263
15	0.861	0.743	0.642	0.555	0.481	0.417	0.362	0.315	0.275	0.239

(n)	11%	12%	13%	14%	15%	16%	17%	18%	19%	20%
1	0.901	0.893	0.885	0.877	0.870	0.862	0.855	0.847	0.840	0.833
2	0.812	0.797	0.783	0.769	0.756	0.743	0.731	0.718	0.706	0.694
3	0.731	0.712	0.693	0.675	0.658	0.641	0.624	0.609	0.593	0.579
4	0.659	0.636	0.613	0.592	0.572	0.552	0.534	0.516	0.499	0.482
5	0.593	0.567	0.543	0.519	0.497	0.476	0.456	0.437	0.419	0.402
6	0.535	0.507	0.480	0.456	0.432	0.410	0.390	0.370	0.352	0.335
7	0.482	0.452	0.425	0.400	0.376	0.354	0.333	0.314	0.296	0.279
8	0.434	0.404	0.376	0.351	0.327	0.305	0.285	0.266	0.249	0.233
9	0.391	0.361	0.333	0.308	0.284	0.263	0.243	0.225	0.209	0.194
10	0.352	0.322	0.295	0.270	0.247	0.227	0.208	0.191	0.176	0.162
11	0.317	0.287	0.261	0.237	0.215	0.195	0.178	0.162	0.148	0.135
12	0.286	0.257	0.231	0.208	0.187	0.168	0.152	0.137	0.124	0.112
13	0.258	0.229	0.204	0.182	0.163	0.145	0.130	0.116	0.104	0.093
14	0.232	0.205	0.181	0.160	0.141	0.125	0.111	0.099	0.088	0.078
15	0.209	0.183	0.160	0.140	0.123	0.108	0.095	0.084	0.079	0.065

KAPLAN PUBLISHING

ANNUITY TABLE

Present value of an annuity of 1 i.e. $\dfrac{1-(1+r)^{-n}}{r}$

Where r = interest rate

         n = number of periods.

Periods (n)	Discount rate (r)									
	1%	**2%**	**3%**	**4%**	**5%**	**6%**	**7%**	**8%**	**9%**	**10%**
1	0.990	0.980	0.971	0.962	0.952	0.943	0.935	0.926	0.917	0.909
2	1.970	1.942	1.913	1.886	1.859	1.833	1.808	1.783	1.759	1.736
3	2.941	2.884	2.829	2.775	2.723	2.673	2.624	2.577	2.531	2.487
4	3.902	3.808	3.717	3.630	3.546	3.465	3.387	3.312	3.240	3.170
5	4.853	4.713	4.580	4.452	4.329	4.212	4.100	3.993	3.890	3.791
6	5.795	5.601	5.417	5.242	5.076	4.917	4.767	4.623	4.486	4.355
7	6.728	6.472	6.230	6.002	5.786	5.582	5.389	5.206	5.033	4.868
8	7.652	7.325	7.020	6.733	6.463	6.210	5.971	5.747	5.535	5.335
9	8.566	8.162	7.786	7.435	7.108	6.802	6.515	6.247	5.995	5.759
10	9.471	8.983	8.530	8.111	7.722	7.360	7.024	6.710	6.418	6.145
11	10.368	9.787	9.253	8.760	8.306	7.887	7.499	7.139	6.805	6.495
12	11.255	10.575	9.954	9.385	8.863	8.384	7.943	7.536	7.161	6.814
13	12.134	11.348	10.635	9.986	9.394	8.853	8.358	7.904	7.487	7.103
14	13.004	12.106	11.296	10.563	9.899	9.295	8.745	8.244	7.786	7.367
15	13.865	12.849	11.938	11.118	10.380	9.712	9.108	8.559	8.061	7.606

(n)	**11%**	**12%**	**13%**	**14%**	**15%**	**16%**	**17%**	**18%**	**19%**	**20%**
1	0.901	0.893	0.885	0.877	0.870	0.862	0.855	0.847	0.840	0.833
2	1.713	1.690	1.668	1.647	1.626	1.605	1.585	1.566	1.547	1.528
3	2.444	2.402	2.361	2.322	2.283	2.246	2.210	2.174	2.140	2.106
4	3.102	3.037	2.974	2.914	2.855	2.798	2.743	2.690	2.639	2.589
5	3.696	3.605	3.517	3.433	3.352	3.274	3.199	3.127	3.058	2.991
6	4.231	4.111	3.998	3.889	3.784	3.685	3.589	3.498	3.410	3.326
7	4.712	4.564	4.423	4.288	4.160	4.039	3.922	3.812	3.706	3.605
8	5.146	4.968	4.799	4.639	4.487	4.344	4.207	4.078	3.954	3.837
9	5.537	5.328	5.132	4.946	4.772	4.607	4.451	4.303	4.163	4.031
10	5.889	5.650	5.426	5.216	5.019	4.833	4.659	4.494	4.339	4.192
11	6.207	5.938	5.687	5.453	5.234	5.029	4.836	4.656	4.486	4.327
12	6.492	6.194	5.918	5.660	5.421	5.197	4.988	7.793	4.611	4.439
13	6.750	6.424	6.122	5.842	5.583	5.342	5.118	4.910	4.715	4.533
14	6.982	6.628	6.302	6.002	5.724	5.468	5.229	5.008	4.802	4.611
15	7.191	6.811	6.462	6.142	5.847	5.575	5.324	5.092	4.876	4.675

Section 1

PRACTICE QUESTIONS

Note: All questions carry two marks

THE NATURE AND PURPOSE OF MANAGEMENT ACCOUNTING

1   **Which of the following statements are correct?**

(i)   Strategic information is mainly used by senior management in an organisation.

(ii)   Productivity measurements are examples of tactical information.

(iii) Operational information is required frequently by its main users.

A   (i) and (ii) only

B   (i) and (iii) only

C   (ii) and (iii) only

D   (i), (ii) and (iii)

2   **Reginald is the manager of production department M in a factory which has ten other production departments.**

He receives monthly information that compares planned and actual expenditure for department M. After department M, all production goes into other factory departments to be completed prior to being despatched to customers. Decisions involving capital expenditure in department M are not taken by Reginald.

Which of the following describes Reginald's role in department M?

A   A cost centre manager

B   An investment centre manager

C   A revenue centre manager

3   **Which of the following is NOT CORRECT?**

A   Cost accounting can be used for inventory valuation to meet the requirements of internal reporting only.

B   Management accounting provides appropriate information for decision making, planning, control and performance evaluation.

C   Routine information can be used for both short-term and long-run decisions.

D   Financial accounting information can be used for internal reporting purposes.

4   The following statements relate to financial accounting or to cost and management accounting:

(i)   Financial accounts are historical records.

(ii)   Cost accounting is part of financial accounting and establishes costs incurred by an organisation.

(iii) Management accounting is used to aid planning, control and decision making.

Which of the statements are correct?

A   (i) and (ii) only

B   (i) and (iii) only

C   (ii) and (iii) only

D   (i), (ii) and (iii)

5   Which of the following is correct?

A   Qualitative data is generally non-numerical information.

B   Information can only be extracted from external sources.

C   Operational information gives details of long-term plans only.

6   The manager of a profit centre is responsible for which of the following?

(i)   Revenues of the centre

(ii)   Costs of the centre

(iii) Assets employed in the centre

A   (i) only

B   (ii) only

C   (i) and (ii) only

D   (i), (ii) and (iii)

7   Which of the following would be best described as a short-term tactical plan?

A   Reviewing cost variances and investigate as appropriate

B   Comparing actual market share to budget

C   Lowering the selling price by 15%

D   Monitoring actual sales to budget

8   The following statements refer to strategic planning:

(i)   It is concerned with quantifiable and qualitative matters.

(ii)   It is mainly undertaken by middle management in an organisation.

(iii) It is concerned predominantly with the long term.

Which of the statements are correct?

A   (i) and (ii) only

B   (i) and (iii) only

C   (ii) and (iii) only

D   (i), (ii) and (iii)

9   **The following statements relate to responsibility centres:**

(i)   Return on capital employed is a suitable measure of performance in both profit and investment centres.

(ii)   Cost centres are found in manufacturing organisations but not in service organisations.

(iii)   The manager of a revenue centre is responsible for both sales and costs in a part of an organisation.

Which of the statements are incorrect?

A   (i) and (ii)

B   (ii) and (iii)

C   All of them

10   **A paint manufacturer has a number of departments. Each department is located in a separate building on the same factory site. In the mixing department the basic raw materials are mixed together in very large vessels. These are then moved on to the colour adding department where paints of different colours are created in these vessels. In the next department – the pouring department – the paint is poured from these vessels into litre sized tins. The tins then go on to the labelling department prior to going on to the finished goods department.**

The following statements relate to the paint manufacturer:

(i)   The mixing department is a cost centre.

(ii)   A suitable cost unit for the colour adding department is a litre tin of paint.

(iii)   The pouring department is a profit centre.

Which statement or statements is/are correct?

A   (i) only

B   (i) and (ii) only

C   (i) and (iii) only

D   (ii) and (iii) only

SOURCES OF DATA

11   **The following statements refer to qualities of good information:**

(i)   It should be communicated to the right person.

(ii)   It should always be completely accurate before it is used.

(iii)   It should be understandable by the recipient.

Which of the above statements are correct?

A   (i) and (ii) only

B   (i) and (iii) only

C   (ii) and (iii) only

D   (i), (ii) and (iii)

12 The essence of systematic sampling is that:

A   each element of the population has an equal chance of being chosen

B   members of various strata are selected by the interviewers up to predetermined limits

C   every nth member of the population is selected

D   every element of one definable sub-section of the population is selected

13 A firm which bottles shampoo selects some filled bottles for examination. The procedure used is that two random numbers, x and y, are chosen. Starting at the xth bottle filled, every bottle at an interval of y is then chosen for examination.

This type of sampling is known as:

A   Multi-stage

B   Random

C   Systematic

D   Stratified

14 The following statements are often made about 'simple random sampling'.

(i)   It ensures a representative sample.

(ii)   It eliminates selection bias.

Which of the following is always true?

A   (i) only

B   (ii) only

C   Both (i) and (ii)

D   Neither (i) nor (ii)

15 An accountant has to check a sample of invoices. The invoices are divided into three groups, by value as follows: 'under £100', '£100 - £500' and 'over £500'. Samples are then selected randomly from each group.

Which ONE of the following sampling methods is involved?

A   Cluster

B   Multi-stage

C   Quota

D   Stratified

16 A sample of 10% of ACCA students is required. Which ONE of the following methods will provide the best simple random sample?

A   Select every tenth ACCA student to arrive at their college/institute on one specific day

B   Select randomly, using random number tables, one in ten of every ACCA class

C   Select 10% of colleges/institutions providing ACCA courses, then from these choose all students who are registered with ACCA

D   Select 10% of all students registered with ACCA, giving each a chance of 0.1 of being picked

PRESENTING INFORMATION

17 The following table shows that the typical salary of part qualified accountants in five different regions of England.

Area	Typical salary £
South-east	21,500
Midlands	20,800
North-east	18,200
North-west	17,500
South-west	16,700

The best diagram to draw to highlight the differences between areas is:

A   a pie diagram

B   a multiple bar chart

C   a percentage component bar chart

D   a simple bar chart

18 A line graph is being produced to show the cost of advertising and sales revenue for a business. Which values would be shown on which axis?

A   Both on the y-axis

B   Both on the x-axis

C   Cost of advertising on the x-axis and sales revenue on the y-axis

D   Sales revenue on the x-axis and cost of advertising on the y-axis

19 A pie chart is being produced to represent the sales from different regional offices of a business:

	$000
North	125
North West	180
East	241
South	691
South East	147
Total	1,384

What would be the angle of the East divisions section on the pie chart (to the nearest whole degree)?

A   63°

B   33°

C   180°

D   58°

20   The overhead cost a business has been allocated and apportioned into the different cost centres. A pie chart has been used to present this information. The assembly department is represented by a section that has an angle of 45°. The total overhead cost is $800,000.

What is the value of the overhead that has been allocated and apportioned to assembly?

A $360,000

B $100,000

C $120,000

D $640,000

TYPES OF COST AND COST BEHAVIOUR

21   The following diagram represents the behaviour of one element of cost:

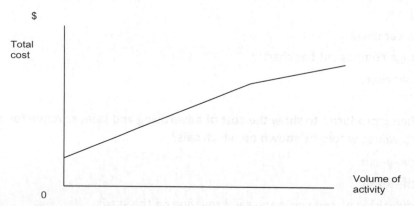

Which one of the following descriptions is consistent with the above diagram?

A   Annual total cost of factory power where the supplier sets a tariff based on a fixed charge plus a constant unit cost for consumption which is subject to a maximum annual charge.

B   Total annual direct material cost where the supplier charges a constant amount per unit which then reduces to a lower amount per unit after a certain level of purchases.

C   Total annual direct material cost where the supplier charges a constant amount per unit but when purchases exceed a certain level a lower amount per unit applies to all purchases in the year.

D   Annual total cost of telephone services where the supplier makes a fixed charge and then a constant unit rate for calls up to a certain level. This rate then reduces for all calls above this level.

22   An organisation has the following total costs at three activity levels:

Activity level (units)	8,000	12,000	15,000
Total cost	$204,000	$250,000	$274,000

Variable cost per unit is constant within this activity range and there is a step up of 10% in the total fixed costs when the activity level exceeds 11,000 units.

What is the total cost at an activity level of 10,000 units?

A $220,000

B $224,000

C $227,000

D $234,000

23 A firm has to pay a $0.50 per unit royalty to the inventor of a device which it manufactures and sells.

The royalty charge would be classified in the firm's accounts as a:

A   selling expense

B   direct expense

C   production overhead

D   administrative overhead.

24 Inventory is valued at total cost per unit.

Is this statement true or false?

A   True

B   False

25 Which of the following is usually classed as a step cost?

A   Supervisor's wages

B   Raw materials

C   Rates

D   Telephone

26 All of the following may be cost objects except:

A   a cost centre

B   a customer

C   a manager

D   a product.

27 Depreciation of fixtures is:

A   not a cash cost so is ignored in the cost accounts

B   part of manufacturing overheads

C   part of prime cost.

28 Which ONE of the following costs would NOT be classified as a production overhead cost in a food processing company?

A   The cost of renting the factory building

B   The salary of the factory manager

C   The depreciation of equipment located in the materials store

D   The cost of ingredients

29 The prime cost of a product is the sum of the labour and materials costs that are identifiable to individual units of the product.

This statement is:

A   True

B   False

30 There is to be an increase next year in the rent for a warehouse used to store finished goods ready for sale. The impact of this increase on the value of inventory manufactured next year and held in the warehouse will be:

A   an increase

B   a decrease

C   no change.

31 The diagram represents the behaviour of a cost item as the level of output changes:

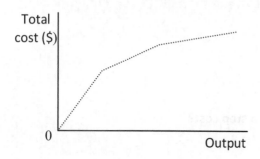

Which ONE of the following situations is described by the graph?

A   Discounts are received on additional purchases of material when certain quantities are purchased.

B   Employees are paid a guaranteed weekly wage, together with bonuses for higher levels of production.

C   A licence is purchased from the government that allows unlimited production.

D   Additional space is rented to cope with the need to increase production.

32 Which ONE of the following would be classified as direct labour?

A   Personnel manager in a company servicing cars

B   Bricklayer in a construction company

C   General manager in a DIY shop

D   Maintenance manager in a company producing cameras

33 Cost centres are:

A   units of product or service for which costs are ascertained

B   amounts of expenditure attributable to various activities

C   functions or locations for which costs are ascertained

D   a section of an organisation for which budgets are prepared and control exercised.

34 The following data relate to two output levels of a department:

Machine hours	17,000	18,500
Overheads	$246,500	$251,750

The amount of fixed overheads is:

A $5,250

B $59,500

C $187,000

D $246,500

35 **A kitchen fitting company receives an invoice for sub-contractors who were used to connect the gas supply to a cooker installed in a new kitchen.**

How would this invoice be classified?

A   Direct expenses

B   Indirect expenses

C   Direct labour

D   Indirect labour

36 **A manufacturing company has four types of cost (identified as T1, T2 , T3 and T4).**

The total cost for each type at two different production levels is:

Cost type	Total cost for 125 units $	Total cost for 180 units $
T1	1,000	1,260
T2	1,750	2,520
T3	2,475	2,826
T4	3,225	4,644

Which two cost types would be classified as being semi-variable?

A   T1 and T3

B   T1 and T4

C   T2 and T3

D   T2 and T4

37 **The following data relate to the overhead expenditure of contract cleaners at two activity levels:**

Square metres cleaned	12,750	15,100
Overheads	$73,950	$83,585

Using the high-low method, what is the estimate of the overhead cost if 16,200 square metres are to be cleaned?

A $88,095

B $89,674

C $93,960

D $98,095

38 **A company manufactures and sells toys and incurs the following three costs:**

(i)   Rental of the finished goods warehouse

(ii)   Depreciation of its own fleet of delivery vehicles

(iii)   Commission paid to sales staff.

Which of these are classified as distribution costs?

A   (i) and (ii) only

B   (ii) and (iii) only

C   (ii) and (iii) only.

D   (i), (ii) and (iii).

39 A company incurs the following costs at various activity levels:

Total cost	Activity level
$	Units
250,000	5,000
312,500	7,500
400,000	10,000

Using the high-low method what is the variable cost per unit?

A $25

B $30

C $35

D $40

40 An organisation manufactures a single product. The total cost of making 4,000 units is $20,000 and the total cost of making 20,000 units is $40,000. Within this range of activity the total fixed costs remain unchanged.

What is the variable cost per unit of the product?

A $0.80

B $1.20

C $1.25

D $2.00

41 The total materials cost of a company is such that when total purchases exceed 15,000 units in any period, then all units purchased, including the first 15,000, are invoiced at a lower cost per unit.

Determine which of the following graphical representations is consistent with the behaviour of the total materials cost in a period.

A

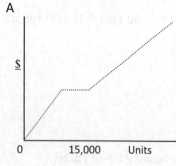

B

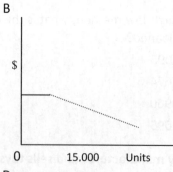

C

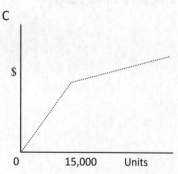

D

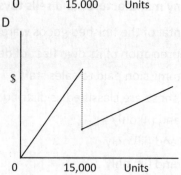

42 A supplier of telephone services charges a fixed line rental per period. The first 10 hours of telephone calls by the customer are free, after that all calls are charged at a constant rate per minute up to a maximum, thereafter all calls in the period are again free.

Which of the following graphs depicts the total cost to the customer of the telephone services in a period?

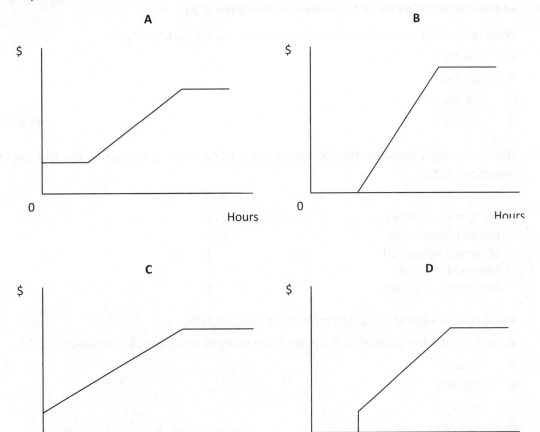

43 The following production and total cost information relates to a single product organisation for the last three months:

Month	Production units	Total cost $
1	1,200	66,600
2	900	58,200
3	1,400	68,200

The variable cost per unit is constant up to a production level of 2,000 units per month but a step up of $6,000 in the monthly total fixed cost occurs when production reaches 1,100 units per month.

What is the total cost for a month when 1,000 units are produced?

A $54,200

B $55,000

C $59,000

D $60,200

ORDERING AND ACCOUNTING FOR INVENTORY

44 A manufacturing company uses 28,000 components at an even rate during the year. Each order placed with the supplier of the components is for 1,500 components, which is the economic order quantity. The company holds a buffer inventory of 700 components. The annual cost of holding one component in inventory is $3.

What is the total annual cost of holding inventory of the component?

A $2,250

B $3,300

C $4,350

D $4,500   (2 marks)

45 The following represent the materials transactions for a company for the month of December 20X6:

	$000s
Materials purchases	176
Issued to production	165
Materials written off	4
Returned to stores	9
Returned to suppliers	8

The material inventory at 1 December 20X6 was $15,000.

What is the closing balance on the materials inventory account at 31 December 20X6?

A $5,000

B $16,000

C $23,000

D $31,000

46 Which of the following statements is correct?

A   A stores ledger account will be updated from a goods received note only.

B   A stores requisition will only detail the type of product required by a customer.

C   The term 'lead time' is best used to describe the time between receiving an order and paying for it.

D   To make an issue from stores authorisation should be required.

47 Perpetual inventory is the counting and valuing of selected items on a rotating basis.

This statement is:

A   True

B   False

48 The double entry for an issue of indirect production materials would be:

A   Dr Materials control account   Cr Finished goods control account

B   Dr Production overhead control a/c   Cr Materials control account

C   Dr Work-in-progress control account   Cr Production overhead control a/c

D   Dr Work-in-progress control account   Cr Materials control account

49 **Which of the following will be completed by a production department requiring new materials to be obtained from suppliers?**

A   A purchase order

B   A delivery note

C   A purchase requisition

D   A goods received note

50 **The following represent transactions on the material account for a company for the month of March 20X8:**

	$000s
Issued to production	144
Returned to stores	5

The material inventory at 1 March 20X8 was $23,000 and at 31 March 20X8 was $15,000.

How much material was purchased in March 20X8?

A $131,000

B $139,000

C $141,000

D $159,000

51 **Which of the following procedures are carried out to minimise losses from inventory?**

(i)   use of standard costs for purchases

(ii)   restricted access to stores

(iii)   regular stocktaking

A   (i) and (ii)

B   (ii) and (iii)

C   (ii) only

D   All of them

52 **Appleby buys and sells inventory during the month of August as follows:**

Opening inventory		100 units	$2.52/unit
4 August	Sales	20 units	
8 August	Purchases	140 units	$2.56/unit
10 August	Sales	90 units	
18 August	Purchases	200 units	$2.78/unit
20 August	Sales	180 units	

The periodic weighted average for the month is calculated as follows:

Total value of inventory (opening inventory plus purchase costs during the month) divided by total units (opening inventory plus purchase costs during the month).

Which of the following statements is true?

A   Closing inventory is $19.50 higher when using the FIFO method instead of the periodic weighted average

B   Closing inventory is $19.50 lower when using the FIFO method instead of the periodic weighted average

C   Closing inventory is $17.50 higher when using the FIFO method instead of the periodic weighted average

D   Closing inventory is $17.50 lower when using the FIFO method instead of the periodic weighted average

53   In the year ended 31 August 20X4, Aplus' records show closing inventory of 1,000 units compared to 950 units of opening inventory. Which of the following statements is true assuming that prices have fallen throughout the year?

A   Closing inventory and profit are higher using FIFO rather than AVCO.

B   Closing inventory and profit are lower using FIFO rather than AVCO.

C   Closing inventory is higher and profit lower using FIFO rather than AVCO.

D   Closing inventory is lower and profit higher using FIFO rather than AVCO.

54   Inventory movements for product X during the last quarter were as follows:

January	Purchases	10 items at $19.80 each
February	Sales	10 items at $30 each
March	Purchases	20 items at $24.50
	Sales	5 items at $30 each

Opening inventory at 1 January was 6 items valued at $15 each.

Gross profit for the quarter, using the weighted average cost method, would be:

A $135.75

B $155.00

C $174.00

D $483.00

55   Your firm values inventory using the weighted average cost method. At 1 October 20X8, there were 60 units in inventory valued at $12 each. On 8 October, 40 units were purchased for $15 each, and a further 50 units were purchased for $18 each on 14 October. On 21 October, 75 units were sold for $1,200.

The value of closing inventory at 31 October 20X8 was:

A $900

B $1,020

C $1,110

D $1,125

56 An organisation's inventory at 1 July is 15 units at $3.00 each. The following movements occur:

3 July 20X4	5 units sold at $3.30 each
8 July 20X4	10 units bought at $3.50 each
12 July 20X4	8 units sold at $4.00 each

Closing inventory at 31 July, using the FIFO method of inventory valuation, would be

A $31.50

B $36.00

C $39.00

D $41.00

57 In times of rising prices, the valuation of inventory using the First In First Out method, as opposed to the Weighted Average Cost method, will result in which ONE of the following combinations?

	Cost of sales	Profit	Closing inventory
A	Lower	Higher	Higher
B	Lower	Higher	Lower
C	Higher	Lower	Higher
D	Higher	Higher	Lower

ORDER QUANTITIES AND REORDER LEVELS

58 A company determines its order quantity for a component using the Economic Order Quantity (EOQ) model.

What would be the effects on the EOQ and the total annual ordering cost of an increase in the annual cost of holding one unit of the component in inventory?

	EOQ	Total annual ordering cost
A	Lower	Higher
B	Higher	Lower
C	Lower	No effect
D	Higher	No effect

59 A company uses the Economic Order Quantity (EOQ) model to establish reorder quantities. The following information relates to the forthcoming period:

Order costs = $25 per order

Holding costs = 10% of purchase price = $4/unit

Annual demand = 20,000 units

Purchase price = $40 per unit

EOQ = 500 units

No safety inventory is held.

What are the total annual costs of inventory (i.e. the total purchase cost plus total order cost plus total holding cost)?

A $22,000

B $33,500

C $802,000

D $803,000

60 Data relating to a particular stores item are as follows:

Average daily usage	400 units
Maximum daily usage	520 units
Minimum daily usage	180 units
Lead time for replenishment of inventory	10 to 15 days
Reorder quantity	8,000 units

What is the reorder level (in units) that avoids inventory stockouts?

A 5,000

B 6,000

C 7,800

D 8,000

61 A large store selling office furniture stocks a popular chair for which the following information is available:

Annual demand:	4,000 chairs
Maximum inventory:	75 chairs
Minimum inventory:	20 chairs
Lead time:	5 days
Re-order quantity:	100 chairs

What is the average inventory level?

A 75 chairs

B 70 chairs

C 55 chairs

D 47 chairs

62 What is the economic batch quantity used to establish?

Optimal

A reorder quantity

B reorder level

C maximum inventory levels

D quantity to be manufactured.

63   A company manufactures a product in batches and then holds the items produced in finished goods inventory until they are sold. It is capable of replenishing the product at the rate of 100,000 units/year, but annual sales demand is just 40,000 units. The cost of setting up a batch production run is $1,500 and the cost of holding a unit of the product in inventory is $25/year.

What is the economic batch quantity for manufacturing this product?

A   2,191 units

B   2,828 units

C   4,472 units

D   10,954 units

64   Which of the following are included in the cost of holding inventory?

(i)   The cost of insurance

(ii)   Rental payments on storage space

(iii)   The cost of placing an order

A   (i) and (ii)

B   (i) and (iii)

C   (ii) and (iii)

D   (i), (ii) and (iii)

65   A manufacturing company uses 25,000 components at an even rate during a year. Each order placed with the supplier of the components is for 2,000 components, which is the economic order quantity. The company holds a buffer inventory of 500 components. The annual cost of holding one component in inventory is $2.

What is the total annual cost of holding inventory of the component?

A $2,000

B $2,500

C $3,000

D $4,000

66   The purchase price of an inventory item is $42 per unit. In each three-month period the usage of the item is 2,000 units. The annual holding costs associated with one unit is 5% of its purchase price. The EOQ is 185 units.

What is the cost of placing an order?

A $4.49

B $11.24

C $17.97

D $35.93

The following information applies to questions 67, 68 and 69

Point uses the economic order quantity (EOQ) model to establish the reorder quantity for raw material Y. The company holds no buffer inventory. Information relating to raw material Y is as follows:

Annual usage	48,000 units
Purchase price	$80 per unit
Ordering costs	$120 per order
Annual holding costs	10% of the purchase price

67   The EOQ for raw material Y is:

A   438

B   800

C   1,200

D   3,795

68   The total annual cost of purchasing, ordering and holding inventory of raw material Y is:

A $3,849,600

B $3,850,400

C $3,853,600

D $3,854,400

69   The supplier has offered Point a discount of 1% on the purchase price if each order placed is for 2,000 units.

The total annual saving to Point of accepting this offer is:

A $29,280

B $30,080

C $37,200

D $38,000

70   A company uses components at the rate of 600 units per month, which are bought in at a cost of $2.24 each from the supplier. It costs $8.75 each time to place an order, regardless of the quantity ordered. The supplier offers a 5% discount on the purchase price for order quantities of 2,000 items or more. The current EOQ is 750 units. The total holding cost is 10% per annum of the value of inventory held.

What is the change in total cost to the company of moving to an order quantity of 2,000 units?

A $601 additional cost

B $730 additional cost

C $730 saving

D $601 saving

71   A company makes a component for one of its products in-house. It uses an average of 5,000 of these throughout the year. The production rate for these components is 500 per week and the cost of holding one item for the year is $1.50. The factory is open for 50 weeks per year. The company has calculated that the economic batch quantity is 2,000. What is the production setup cost per batch?

A $213

B $240

C $480

D $960

ACCOUNTING FOR LABOUR

72   The following statements relate to labour costs:

There would be an increase in the total cost for labour as a result of:

(i)   additional labour being employed on a temporary basis

(ii)   a department with spare capacity being made to work more hours

(iii)   a department which is at full capacity switching from the production of one product to another.

Which of the above is/are correct?

A   (i) only

B   (ii) only

C   (iii) only

D   (i) and (iii) only

73   A manufacturing firm is very busy and overtime is being worked.

The amount of overtime premium contained in direct wages would normally be classed as:

A   part of prime cost

B   factory overheads

C   direct labour costs

D   administrative overheads.

74   KL currently pays its direct production workers on a time basis at a rate of $6.50 per hour. In an effort to improve productivity, the company is introducing a bonus based on (time taken/time allowed) × time saved × rate per hour. The standard time allowed for a worker in the Assembly Department to perform this particular operation once has been agreed at 37.5 minutes.

In the first week of the scheme's operation, one employee worked for a total of 44 hours and performed 94 operations.

The gross wages for this employee based on a time rate of $6.50 per hour plus the productivity bonus based on (time taken/time allowed) × time saved × rate per hour, to 2 decimal places, is:

A $214.20

B $357.80

C $381.88

D $977.60

75 If the direct labour costs in a manufacturing company are $95,000 in March, the costs would be recorded in the cost ledger as:

A   Debit Work-in-progress $95,000, Credit Wages and salaries $95,000

B   Debit Wages and salaries $95,000, Credit Bank $95,000

C   Debit Wages and salaries $95,000, Credit Work-in-progress $95,000

D   Debit Bank $95,000, Credit Wages and salaries $95,000

76 Budgeted production in a factory for next period is 4,800 units. Each unit requires five labour hours to make. Labour is paid $10 per hour. Idle time represents 20% of the total labour time.

What is the budgeted total labour cost for the next period?

A $192,000

B $240,000

C $288,000

D $300,000

77 The following statements refer to situations occurring in Process Q of an organisation which operates a series of consecutive processes:

(i)   Direct labour is working at below the agreed productivity level.

(ii)   A machine breakdown has occurred.

(iii)   Direct labour is waiting for work to be completed in a previous process.

Which of these situations could give rise to idle time?

A   (i) and (ii) only

B   (i) and (iii) only

C   (ii) and (iii) only

D   (i), (ii) and (iii)

78 A direct labour employee works a standard 37 hour week and is paid a basic rate of $15 per hour. Overtime is paid at time and a half. In a week when 40 hours were worked and a bonus of $20 was paid, what was the direct labour cost?

A $555

B $600

C $622.50

D $642.50

79 At 1 January a company employed 5,250 employees. Due to expansion the number of employees increased to 5,680 by 31 December. During the year 360 staff left the company and were replaced. What was the labour turnover rate?

A   6.3%

B   6.6%

C   6.9%

D   360 staff

The following information applies to questions 80, 81 and 82

A company records the following information concerning a product:

Standard time allowed per unit	16 minutes
Actual output in period	720 units
Actual hours worked	180
Budgeted hours	185

80   What is the labour efficiency ratio?

A   93.75%

B   97.3%

C   102.5%

D   106.7%

81   What is the labour capacity ratio?

A   102.8%

B   99.4%

C   98.6%

D   97.3%

82   What is the production volume ratio?

A   97.3%

B   102.5%

C   103.8%

D   106.7%

ACCOUNTING FOR OVERHEADS

83   A factory consists of two production cost centres (G and H) and two service cost centres (J and K). The total overheads allocated and apportioned to each centre are as follows:

G	H	J	K
$40,000	$50,000	$30,000	$18,000

The work done by the service cost centres can be represented as follows:

	G	H	J	K
Percentage of service cost centre J to	30%	70%	–	–
Percentage of service cost centre K to	50%	40%	10%	–

The company apportions service cost centre costs to production cost centres using a method that fully recognises any work done by one service cost centre for another.

What are the total overheads for production cost centre G after the reapportionment of all service cost centre costs?

A $58,000

B $58,540

C $59,000

D $59,540

84 An overhead absorption rate is used to:

A share out common costs over benefiting cost centres

B find the total overheads for a cost centre

C charge overheads to products

D control overheads.

85 A factory consists of two production cost centres (P and Q) and two service cost centres (X and Y). The total allocated and apportioned overhead for each is as follows:

P	Q	X	Y
$95,000	$82,000	$46,000	$30,000

It has been estimated that each service cost centre does work for the other cost centres in the following proportions:

	P	Q	X	Y
Percentage of service cost centre X to	40	40	–	20
Percentage of service cost centre Y to	30	60	10	–

After the reapportionment of service cost centre costs has been carried out using a method that fully recognises the reciprocal service arrangements in the factory, what is the total overhead for production cost centre P?

A $122,400

B $124,716

C $126,000

D $127,000

86 A cost centre has an overhead absorption rate of $4.25 per machine hour, based on a budgeted activity level of 12,400 machine hours.

In the period covered by the budget, actual machine hours worked were 2% more than the budgeted hours and the actual overhead expenditure incurred in the cost centre was $56,389.

What was the total over or under absorption of overheads in the cost centre for the period?

A $1,054 over absorbed

B $2,635 under absorbed

C $3,689 over absorbed

D $3,689 under absorbed

87 Over-absorbed overheads occur when:

A absorbed overheads exceed actual overheads

B absorbed overheads exceed budgeted overheads

C actual overheads exceed budgeted overheads

D budgeted overheads exceed absorbed overheads.

88 The management accountant's report shows that fixed production overheads were over-absorbed in the last accounting period. The combination that is certain to lead to this situation is:

A production volume is lower than budget and actual expenditure is higher than budget

B production volume is higher than budget and actual expenditure is higher than budget

C production volume and actual cost are as budgeted

D production volume is higher than budget and actual expenditure is lower than budget.

89   At the end of a period, in an integrated cost and financial accounting system, the accounting entries for $10,000 overheads over-absorbed would be:

A	Dr	Work-in-progress control account	Cr	Overhead control account
B	Dr	Income statement	Cr	Work-in-progress control account
C	Dr	Income statement	Cr	Overhead control account
D	Dr	Overhead control account	Cr	Income statement

90   During a period $50,000 was incurred for indirect labour. In a typical cost ledger, the double entry for this is:

A	Dr	Wages control	Cr	Overhead control
B	Dr	WIP control	Cr	Wages control
C	Dr	Overhead control	Cr	Wages control
D	Dr	Wages control	Cr	WIP control

91   Iddon makes two products, Pye and Tan, in a factory divided into two production departments, machining and assembly. In order to find a fixed overhead cost per unit, the following budgeted data are relevant.

	Machining	Assembly
Direct and allocated fixed costs	$120,000	$72,000
Labour hours per unit		
Pye	0.50 hour	0.20 hour
Tan	1.00 hour	0.25 hour

Budgeted production is 4,000 units of each product (8,000 units in all) and fixed overheads are to be absorbed by reference to labour hours.

What is the budgeted fixed overhead cost of a unit of Pye?

A $18

B $20

C $24

D $28

92   What is cost apportionment?

A   The charging of discrete identifiable items of cost to cost centres or cost units.

B   The collection of costs attributable to cost centres and cost units using the costing methods, principles and techniques prescribed for a particular business entity.

C   The process of establishing the costs of cost centres or cost units.

D   The division of costs amongst two or more cost centres in proportion to the estimated benefit received, using a proxy, e.g. square feet.

93 A law firm recovers overheads on chargeable consulting hours. Budgeted overheads were $615,000 and actual consulting hours were 32,150. Overheads were under-recovered by $35,000.

If actual overheads were $694,075, the budgeted overhead absorption rate per hour is (to 2 decimal places):

A $20.21

B $20.50

C $21.59

D $22.68

94 A finishing department absorbs production overheads using a direct labour hour basis. Budgeted production overheads for the year just ended were $268,800 for the department, and actual production overhead costs were $245,600.

If actual labour hours worked were 45,000 and production overheads were over-absorbed by $6,400, what was the overhead absorption rate per labour hour?

A $5.32

B $5.60

C $5.83

D $6.12

95 A firm absorbs overheads on labour hours. In one period 11,500 hours were worked, actual overheads were $138,000 and there was $23,000 over-absorption. The overhead absorption rate per hour was:

A $10

B $12

C $13

D $14

96 A factory has two production departments, X and Y, and two service departments C and D.

The following information costs relates to the overhead costs in each department.

	Manufacturing departments		Service departments	
	X	Y	C	D
Overhead costs	$5,000	$7,500	$3,200	$4,600
Proportion of usage of services of C	50%	40%	–	10%
Proportion of usage of services of D	20%	60%	20%	–

Using the reciprocal method of apportioning service department costs, the total overhead costs allocated to department X will be:

A $5,000

B $7,520

C $8,105

D $12,195

97 The following budgeted and actual results relate to production activity and overhead costs in WX.

	Budget	Actual
Production overhead costs		
Fixed	$36,000	$39,000
Variable	$9,000	$12,000
Direct labour hours worked	18,000 hours	20,000 hours

An absorption costing system is used and production overhead costs are absorbed into output costs on a direct labour hour basis.

The total production overhead (both fixed and variable) during the period was:

A over-absorbed by $1,000

B under-absorbed by $1,000

C under-absorbed by $5,000

D under-absorbed by $6,000.

98 Lerna produces hydras in three production departments and needs to apportion budgeted monthly fixed costs between those departments. Budgeted costs are as follows:

	$
Rent	2,000
Rates	1,000
Plant insurance	1,000
Plant depreciation	10,000
Supervisor's salary	7,000
	21,000

The following additional information is available.

	Department A	Department B	Department C
Area (square feet)	3,800	3,500	700
Value of machinery ($000)	210	110	80
Number of employees	34	16	20

The total budgeted monthly fixed overhead cost for Department C is:

A $1,837.50

B $4,462.50

C $7,000.00

D $10,600.00

99 The following information is available regarding the fixed overhead costs and output of the two production departments of a firm.

Department	S	T
Allocated or apportioned fixed overhead	$60,000	$100,000
Total cost of direct materials used	$120,000	$100,000
Total productive labour hours	5,000	10,000

A particular product has the following variable cost.

				$
Materials				
Department S	3 kg	@	$4 per kg	12
Department T	2 kg	@	$4 per kg	8
Labour				
Department S	½ hour	@	$10 per hour	5
Department T	1½ hours	@	$10 per hour	15
Variable overheads	1 hour	@	$5 per hour	5
				45

If fixed overheads are absorbed on the basis of departmental material cost, the fixed overhead cost per unit is:

A $5.50

B $12.00

C $14.00

D $21.00

MARGINAL AND ABSORPTION COSTING

100 PQR sells one product. The cost card for that product is given below:

	$
Direct materials	4
Direct labour	5
Variable production overhead	3
Fixed production overhead	2
Variable selling cost	3

The selling price per unit is $20. Budgeted fixed overheads are based on budgeted production of 1,000 units. Opening inventory was 200 units and closing inventory was 150 units. Sales during the period were 800 units and actual fixed overheads incurred were $1,500.

The total contribution earned during the period was:

A $2000

B $2,500

C $4,000

D $2,500

101 E operates a marginal costing system. For the forthcoming year, variable costs are budgeted to be 60% of sales value and fixed costs are budgeted to be 10% of sales value.

If E increases its selling prices by 10%, but if fixed costs, variable costs per unit and sales volume remain unchanged, the effect on E's contribution would be:

A   a decrease of 2%

B   an increase of 5%

C   an increase of 10%

D   an increase of 25%.

102 Last month a manufacturing company's profit was $2,000, calculated using absorption costing principles. If marginal costing principles had been used, a loss of $3,000 would have occurred. The company's fixed production cost is $2 per unit. Sales last month were 10,000 units.

What was last month's production (in units)?

A   7,500

B   9,500

C   10,500

D   12,500

103 A company produces and sells a single product whose variable cost is $6 per unit.

Fixed costs have been absorbed over the normal level of activity of 200,000 units and have been calculated as $2 per unit.

The current selling price is $10 per unit.

How much profit is made under marginal costing if the company sells 250,000 units?

A $500,000

B $600,000

C $900,000

D $1,000,000

104 A company manufactures and sells a single product. For this month the budgeted fixed production overheads are $48,000, budgeted production is 12,000 units and budgeted sales are 11,720 units.

The company currently uses absorption costing.

If the company used marginal costing principles instead of absorption costing for this month, what would be the effect on the budgeted profit?

A $1,120 higher

B $1,120 lower

C $3,920 higher

D $3,920 lower

105 When opening inventory was 8,500 litres and closing inventory was 6,750 litres, a firm had a profit of $62,100 using marginal costing.

Assuming that the fixed overhead absorption rate was $3 per litre, what would be the profit using absorption costing?

A $41,850

B $56,850

C $67,350

D $82,350

106 A company has established a marginal costing profit of $72,300. Opening inventory was 300 units and closing inventory is 750 units. The fixed production overhead absorption rate has been calculated as $5/unit.

What was the profit under absorption costing?

A $67,050

B $70,050

C $74,550

D $77,550

The following data are for questions 107 and 108

The budget for Bright's first month of trading, producing and selling boats was as follows:

	$000
Variable production cost of boats	45
Fixed production costs	30
Production costs of 750 boats	75
Closing inventory of 250 boats	(25)
Production cost of 500 sold	50
Variable selling costs	5
Fixed selling costs	25
	80
Profit	10
Sales revenue	90

The budget has been produced using an absorption costing system.

---

107 If a marginal costing system were used, the budgeted profit would be:

A $22,500 lower

B $10,000 lower

C $10,000 higher

D $22,500 higher

108 **Assume that at the end of the first month unit variable costs and fixed costs and selling price for the month were in line with the budget and any inventory was valued at the same unit cost as in the above budget.**

However, if production was actually 700 and sales 600, what would be the reported profit using absorption costing?

A $9,000

B $12,000

C $14,000

D $15,000

109 **Which of the following are true of marginal costing?**

(i) The marginal cost of a product includes an allowance for fixed production costs.

(ii) The marginal cost of a product represents the additional cost of producing an extra unit.

(iii) If the inventory increases over a year, the profits under absorption costing will be lower than with marginal costing.

A (i) only

B (ii) only

C (ii) and (iii) only

D (i), (ii) and (iii)

110 **A new company has set up a marginal costing system and has a budgeted contribution for the period of $26,000 based on sales of 13,000 units and production of 15,000 units. This level of production represents the firm's expected long-term level of production. The company's budgeted fixed production costs are $3,000 for the period.**

If the company were to change to an absorption costing system the budgeted profit would be:

A $22,600

B $23,400

C $25,600

D $26,400

111 **Which of these statements are true of marginal costing?**

(i) The contribution per unit will be constant if the sales volume increases.

(ii) There is no under- or over-absorption of overheads.

(iii) Marginal costing does not provide useful information for decision making.

A (i) and (ii) only

B (ii) and (iii) only

C (ii) only

D (i), (ii) and (iii)

112 In a period, a company had opening inventory of 31,000 units of Product G and closing inventory of 34,000 units. Profits based on marginal costing were $850,500 and profits based on absorption costing were $955,500.

If the budgeted fixed costs for the company for the period were $1,837,500, what was the budgeted level of activity?

A   24,300 units

B   27,300 units

C   52,500 units

D   65,000 units

113 In a given period, the production level of an item exactly matches the level of sales. The profit reported will be identical whether marginal or absorption costing is used.

This statement is:

A   True

B   False

114 Consider the following graph for total costs and total revenue:

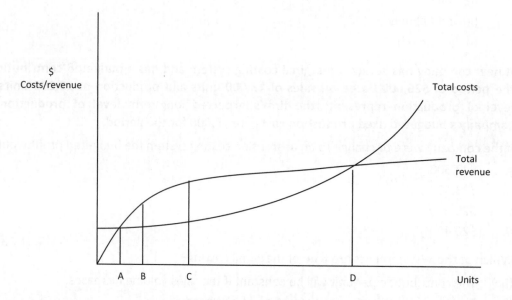

At which point on the above graph is it most likely that profits will be maximised?

A

B

C

D

115 For a product that has a positive unit contribution, which of the following events would tend to increase total contribution by the greatest amount?

A   10% decrease in variable cost.

B   10% increase in selling price.

C   10% increase in volume sold.

D   15% decrease in total fixed costs.

116   Exp has compiled the following standard cost card for its main product.

	$
Production costs	
Fixed	33.00
Variable	45.10
Selling costs	
Fixed	64.00
Variable	7.20
Profit	14.70
Selling price	164.00

Under an absorption costing system, closing inventory would be valued at:

A $52.30

B $78.10

C $97.00

D $149.30

JOB, BATCH AND PROCESS COSTING

117   A company operates a job costing system. Job 812 requires $60 of direct materials, $40 of direct labour and $20 of direct expenses. Direct labour is paid $8 per hour. Production overheads are absorbed at a rate of $16 per direct labour hour and non-production overheads are absorbed at a rate of 60% of prime cost.

What is the total cost of Job 812?

A $240

B $260

C $272

D $320

118   Which one of the following statements is incorrect?

A   Job costs are collected separately, whereas process costs are averages.

B   In job costing the progress of a job can be ascertained from the materials requisition notes and job tickets or time sheet.

C   In process costing information is needed about work passing through a process and work remaining in each process.

D   In process costing, but not job costing, the cost of normal loss will be incorporated into normal product costs.

The following data are to be used for questions 119 and 120

A firm uses job costing and recovers overheads on a direct labour cost basis.

Three jobs were worked on during a period, the details of which were:

	Job 1	Job 2	Job 3
	$	$	$
Opening work-in-progress	8,500	0	46,000
Material in period	17,150	29,025	0
Labour for period	12,500	23,000	4,500

The overheads for the period were exactly as budgeted, $140,000. Actual labour costs were also the same as budgeted.

Jobs 1 and 2 were the only incomplete jobs at the end of the period.

119 **What was the value of closing work-in-progress?**

   A $81,900

   B $90,175

   C $140,675

   D $214,425

120 **Job 3 was completed during the period and consisted of 2,400 identical circuit boards. The firm adds 50% to total production costs to arrive at a selling price.**

   What is the selling price of a circuit board?

   A   It cannot be calculated without more information

   B $31.56

   C $41.41

   D $58.33

121 **A company uses process costing to value output. During the last month the following information was recorded:**

   Output: 2,800 kg valued at $7.50/kg

   Normal loss: 300 kg which has a scrap value of $3/kg

   Actual gain: 100 kg

   What was the value of the input?

   A $22,650

   B $21,900

   C $21,600

   D $21,150

122 ABC manufactures product X in a single process. Normal loss (scrap) in the process is 10% of output and scrapped units can be sold off for $4/unit.

In period 8 there was no opening inventory and no closing inventory. Process costs of direct materials, direct labour and production overheads totalled $184,800. Input to the process in the month was 13,200 units.

What was the cost/unit produced?

A $12.50

B $15.00

C $15.15

D $15.40

123 A company uses process costing to value its output. The following was recorded for the period:

Input materials	2,000 units at $4.50 per unit
Conversion costs	$13,340
Normal loss	5% of input valued at $3 per unit
Abnormal loss	150 units

There were no opening or closing inventories.

What was the valuation of one unit of output?

A $11.80

B $11.60

C $11.20

D $11.00

124 A company that operates a process costing system had work-in-progress at the start of last month of 300 units (valued at $1,710) that were 60% complete in respect of all costs.

Last month a total of 2,000 units were completed and transferred to the finished goods warehouse. The cost per equivalent unit for costs arising last month was $10. The company uses the FIFO method of cost allocation.

What was the total value of the 2,000 units transferred to the finished goods warehouse last month?

A $19,910

B $20,000

C $20,510

D $21,710

125 Vare produces various inks at its Normanton factory. Production details for Process 1 are as follows:

Opening work-in-progress, 1 April	400 units	60% complete
Closing work-in-progress, 30 April	600 units	20% complete
Units started	1,000	
Units finished	800	

The degree of completion quoted relates to labour and overhead costs. Three-quarters of the materials are added at the start of the process and the remaining quarter added when the process is 50% complete. The company uses the FIFO method of cost allocation.

The equivalent units of production for materials in the period are:

- A   1,250
- B   1,000
- C   850
- D   680

126   **Two products W and X are created from a joint process. Both products can be sold immediately after split-off. There are no opening inventories or work-in-progress. The following information is available for the last period:**

Total joint production costs $776,160

Product	Production units	Sales units	Selling Price per unit
W	12,000	10,000	$10
X	10,000	8,000	$12

Using the sales value method of apportioning joint production costs, what was the value of the closing inventory of product X for the last period?

- A $68,992
- B $70,560
- C $76,032
- D $77,616

127   **In a process where there are no work-in-progress inventories, two joint products (J and K) are created. Information (in units) relating to last month is as follows:**

Product	Sales	Opening inventory of finished goods	Closing inventory of finished goods
J	6,000	100	300
K	4,000	400	200

Joint production costs last month were $110,000 and these were apportioned to joint products based on the number of units produced.

What were the joint production costs apportioned to product J for last month?

- A $63,800
- B $64,000
- C $66,000
- D $68,200

128   **Charleville operates a continuous process producing three products and one by-product. Output from the process for a month was as follows:**

Product	Selling price per unit	Units of output from process
1	$18	10,000
2	$25	20,000
3	$20	20,000
4 (by-product)	$2	3,500

Total joint costs were $277,000.

What was the unit cost valuation for product 3 using the sales revenue basis for allocating joint costs assuming that the revenue receivable from the by-product is deducted from the joint costs?

A $4.70

B $4.80

C $5.00

D $5.10

129   A business operates a job costing system and prices its jobs by adding 20% to the total cost of the job. The prime cost of a job was $6,840 and it had used 156 direct labour hours. The fixed production overheads are absorbed on the basis of direct labour hours. The budgeted overhead absorption rate was based upon a budgeted fixed overhead of $300,000 and total budgeted direct labour hours of 60,000.

The job should be sold for:

A $7,620

B $8,208

C $9,144

D $9,525

130   In process costing, if an abnormal loss arises the process account is generally:

A   debited with the scrap value of the abnormal loss units

B   debited with the full production cost of the abnormal loss units

C   credited with the scrap value of the abnormal loss units

D   credited with the full production cost of the abnormal loss units.

131   X uses process costing. In Process 3 the normal loss is 4% of total input.

Last period the input from Process 2 was 8,500 kg and additional material of 4,250 kg was added to process 3.

Actual output to finished goods was 12,700 kg.

There was no opening or closing work-in-progress in the period.

The abnormal gain or loss in kg for period 3 was:

A   460 kg gain

B   460 kg loss

C   290 kg gain

D   290 kg loss

132   A chemical process has a normal wastage of 10% of input. In a period, 2,500 kg of material were input and there was an abnormal loss of 75 kg.

The quantity of good production achieved was:

A   2,175 kg

B   2,250 kg

C   2,325 kg

D   2,675 kg

133 **A company operates a job costing system.**

Job number 605 requires $300 of direct materials and $400 of direct labour. Direct labour is paid at the rate of $8 per hour. Production overheads are absorbed at a rate of $26 per direct labour hour and non-production overheads are absorbed at a rate of 120% of prime cost.

What is the total cost of job number 605?

A $2,000

B $2,400

C $2,840

D $4,400

134 **A factory manufactures model cars. During October work commenced on 110,000 new cars. This was in addition to 20,000 that were 50% complete at the start of the month. At the end of October there were 40,000 cars that were 50% complete.**

Costs for October were:

	$000
Brought forward	11,000
Incurred this period	121,000
	———
	$132,000
	———

If this factory chooses the weighted average method of spreading costs, what is the cost per car for October production?

A $1,100

B $1,200

C $1,210

D $1,320

135 **In a production process the percentage completion of the work-in-progress (WIP) at the end of a period is found to have been understated.**

When this is corrected what will be the effect on the cost per unit and the total value of the WIP?

	Cost per unit	Total value of WIP
A	Decrease	Decrease
B	Decrease	Increase
C	Increase	Decrease
D	Increase	Increase

136 **The following information is available for a production process for the last period:**

Material input	200 kg at $4 per kg
Labour input	100 hours at $15 per hour
Department overhead	$1,000
Transfer to finished goods	150 kg

Normal loss is 10% of input. Losses are identified when the process is 50% complete.

There is no opening or closing work-in-progress.

The total cost of a completed unit is:

A $22.00

B $20.48

C $19.59

D $18.33

137   At the start of the month, there were 2,000 units of work-in-progress in a factory. During the month, 12,000 units were started. At the end of the month, 3,000 units were in closing work in progress. The degree of completion of opening work-in-progress was 70% and closing work in progress was 20%.

How many equivalent units of production were achieved during the month if FIFO were used?

A   10,200

B   11,000

C   11,600

D   14,000

138   The following information is available for a production process for the last period:

Material input	200 kg at $6 per kg
Labour and overhead input	$3,500
Transfer to finished goods	190 kg

Normal loss is 15% of input and has a scrap value of $1 per kg.

There is no opening or closing work-in-progress.

The value of the finished output for the period (to the nearest $) is:

A $4,465

B $4,670

C $5,219

D $5,253

139   Which of the following are features of process costing?

(i)   Homogeneous products

(ii)   Customer-driven production

(iii) Finished goods are valued at an average cost per unit

A   (i) and (iii)

B   (ii) and (iii)

C   (iii) only

D   (i) only

140 A builder has produced a quote for some alterations. The price is made up as follows:

		$
Direct materials	100 kg @ $4 per kg	400
Direct labour	5 hours @ $10 per hour	50
	15 hours @ $5 per hour	75
Hire of machine	1 day @ $100 per day	100
Overheads	20 hours @ $8 per hour	160
		———
Total cost		785
Profit @ 20% of cost	0.2 × $785	157
		———
Price quoted		$942

Actual costs for the job were as follows:

Direct materials	120 kg @ $4 per kg
Direct labour	3 hours @ $10 per hour
	20 hours @ $5 per hour
Hire of machine	2 days @ $100 per day

The actual profit/(loss) made on the job was:

A $52 loss

B $28 loss

C $28 profit

D $52 profit

SERVICE AND OPERATION COSTING

141 Which of the following would be considered a service industry?

(i)   An airline company

(ii)   A railway company

(iii) A firm of accountants

A   (i) and (ii) only

B   (ii) and (iii) only

C   (i), (ii) and (iii)

142 Which of the following are characteristics of service costing?

(i)   High levels of indirect costs as a proportion of total cost.

(ii)   Use of equivalent units.

(iii) Use of composite cost units.

(iv)   Long timescale from commencement to completion of the cost unit.

A   (i) and (iv) only

B   (iii) only

C   (i) and (iii) only

D   All of them

143 Which of the following is NOT likely to be used in a hospital run by a charitable foundation?

A   Cost per patient

B   Cost per bed-day

C   Bed throughput

D   Profit per patient

144 A hotel calculates a number of statistics including average cost per occupied bed per day.

The following information is provided for a 30-day period.

	Rooms with twin beds	Single rooms
Number of rooms in hotel	260	70
Number of rooms available to let	240	40
Average number of rooms occupied daily	200	30

Number of guests in period	6,450
Average length of stay	2 days
Payroll costs for period	$100,000
Cost of cleaning supplies in period	$5,000
Total cost of laundering in period	$22,500

The average cost per occupied bed per day for the period is:

A $9.90

B $9.88

C $7.20

D $8.17

145 The following figures relate to two electricity supply companies.

Meter reading, billing and collection costs

	Company A	Company B
Total cost ($000)	600	1,000
Units sold (millions)	2,880	9,600
Number of consumers (thousands)	800	1,600
Sales of electricity (millions)	$18	$50

The figures given indicate that Company A is more efficient than Company B.

This statement is:

A   True

B   False

146 A hotel calculates a number of statistics including average room occupancy.

Average room occupancy is calculated as the total number of rooms occupied as a percentage of rooms available to let.

The following information is provided for a 30-day period.

	Rooms with twin beds	Single rooms
Number of rooms in hotel	260	70
Number of rooms available to let	240	40
Average number of rooms occupied daily	200	30

The average room occupancy is:

A   69.7%

B   82.1%

C   82.7%

D   84.8%

147 Which of the following are features of service organisations?

(i)   High levels of inventory

(ii)   High proportion of fixed costs

(iii)   Difficulty in identifying suitable cost units

A   (i) and (ii) only

B   (i) and (iii) only

C   (ii) and (iii) only

D   All of these

ALTERNATIVE COSTING PRINCIPLES

148 Which ONE of the following is an advantage of Activity Based Costing?

A   It provides more accurate product costs

B   It is simple to apply

C   It is a form of marginal costing and so is relevant to decision making

D   It is particularly useful when fixed overheads are very low

149 Quality control costs can be categorised into internal and external failure costs, inspection costs and prevention costs. In which of these four classifications would the following costs be included?

- The costs of a customer service team
- The cost of equipment maintenance
- The cost of operating test equipment

	Customer service team	Equipment maintenance	Test equipment
A	Prevention costs	Inspection costs	Internal failure costs
B	Prevention costs	Internal failure costs	Inspection costs
C	External failure costs	Internal failure costs	Prevention costs
D	External failure costs	Prevention costs	Inspection costs

150 In the context of quality costs, customer compensation costs and test equipment running costs would be classified as:

	Customer compensation costs	*Test equipment running costs*
A	Internal failure costs	Prevention costs
B	Internal failure costs	Appraisal costs
C	External failure costs	Appraisal costs
D	External failure costs	Prevention costs

151 The selling price of product K is set at $450 for each unit

If the company requires a return of 20% in the coming year on product K, the target cost for each unit for the coming year is:

A $300

B $360

C $400

D $450

152 In calculating the life cycle costs of a product, which of the following items would be excluded?

(i)   Planning and concept design costs

(ii)   Preliminary and detailed design costs

(iii)   Testing costs

(iv)   Production costs

(v)   Distribution and customer service costs

A   (iii)

B   (iv)

C   (v)

D   None of them

153 As part of a process to achieve a target cost, GYE Inc are interviewing prospective customers to determine why they would buy the product and how they would use it.

What term best describes this process?

A   Value analysis

B   Operational research

C   TQM

D   Lifecycle costing

154 A customer returns a faulty product to a firm for repair under a warranty scheme. The firm operates a total quality management system.

Which of the following best describes the cost of the repair?

A   An internal failure cost

B   An external failure cost

C   An appraisal cost

D   A prevention cost

FORECASTING TECHNIQUES

155 The following information for advertising and sales revenue has been established over the past six months:

Month	Sales revenue	Advertising expenditure
	$000	$000
1	155	3
2	125	2.5
3	200	6
4	175	5.5
5	150	4.5
6	225	6.5

Using the high-low method, which of the following is the correct equation for linking advertising and sales revenue from the above data?

A   Sales revenue = 62,500 + (25 × advertising expenditure)

B   Advertising expenditure = −2,500 + (0.04 × sales revenue)

C   Sales revenue = 95,000 + (20 × advertising expenditure)

D   Advertising expenditure = −4,750 + (0.05 × sales revenue)

156 A company's weekly costs ($C) were plotted against production level (P) for the last 50 weeks and a regression line calculated to be C = 1,000 +250P. Which statement about the breakdown of weekly costs is true?

A   Weekly fixed costs are $1,000, variable costs per unit are $5.

B   Weekly fixed costs are $250, variable costs per unit are $1000.

C   Weekly fixed costs are $1,000, variable costs per unit are $250.

D   Weekly fixed costs are $20, variable costs per unit are $5.

157 If a forecasting model based on total cost = fixed cost + variable costs is graphed, the equation is C = F+Vx and the intercept is $7,788. If total costs are $14,520 and x is 3,300 then the value of the slope, to two decimal places, is:

A   4.40

B   2.04

C   −2.04

D   2.36

158 The correlation coefficient (r) for measuring the connection between two variables (x and y) has been calculated as 0.6.

How much of the variation in the dependent variable (y) is explained by the variation in the independent variable (x)?

A   36%

B   40%

C   60%

D   64%

159 A company uses regression analysis to establish its selling overhead costs for budgeting purposes. The data used for the analysis is as follows:

Month	Number of salesmen	Sales overhead costs $000
1	3	35.1
2	6	46.4
3	4	27.0
4	3	33.5
5	5	41.0
	21	183.0

The gradient of the regression line is 4.20. Using regression analysis, what would be the budgeted sales overhead costs for the month, in $000, if there are 5 salesmen employed?

- A   28.87
- B   39.96
- C   41.00
- D   56.76

160 Which of the following are correct with regard to regression analysis?

(i)   In regression analysis the n stands for the number of pairs of data.

(ii) Σx^2 is not the same calculation as $(\Sigma x)^2$

(iii) Σxy is calculated by multiplying the total value of x and the total value of y

- A   (i) and (ii) only
- B   (i) and (iii) only
- C   (ii) and (iii) only
- D   (i), (ii) and (iii)

161 Regression analysis is being used to find the line of best fit (y = a + bx) from eleven pairs of data. The calculations have produced the following information:

$\Sigma x = 440$, $\Sigma y = 330$, $\Sigma x^2 = 17,986$, $\Sigma y^2 = 10,366$ and $\Sigma xy = 13,467$

What is the value of 'b' in the equation for the line of best fit (to 2 decimal places)?

- A   0.63
- B   0.69
- C   2.33
- D   5.33

An organisation is using linear regression analysis to establish an equation that shows a relationship between advertising expenditure and sales revenue. It will then use the equation to predict sales revenue for given levels of advertising expenditure. Data for the last five periods are as follows:

Period number	Advertising expenditure $000	Sales revenue $000
1	17	108
2	19	116
3	24	141
4	22	123
5	18	112

What are the values of 'Σx', 'Σy' and 'n' that need to be inserted into the appropriate formula?

	Σx	Σy	n
A	$600,000	$100,000	5
B	$100,000	$600,000	5
C	$600,000	$100,000	10
D	$100,000	$600,000	10

163 The coefficient of determination (r^2) has been calculated as 60%.

What does this mean?

A 60% of the variation in the dependent variable (y) is explained by the variation in the independent variable (x)

B 40% of the variation in the dependent variable (y) is explained by the variation in the independent variable (x)

C 60% of the variation in the dependent variable (x) is explained by the variation in the independent variable (y)

D 40% of the variation in the dependent variable (x) is explained by the variation in the independent variable (y)

164 A company has recorded its total cost for different levels of activity over the last five months as follows:

Month	Activity level (units)	Total cost ($)
7	300	17,500
8	360	19,500
9	400	20,500
10	320	18,500
11	280	17,000

The equation for total cost is being calculated using regression analysis on the above data. The equation for total cost is of the general form '$y = a + bx$' and the value of 'b' has been calculated correctly as 29.53.

What is the value of 'a' (to the nearest $) in the total cost equation?

A 7,338

B 8,796

C 10,430

D 10,995

165 Which of the following correlation coefficients indicates the weakest relationship between two variables?

A   + 1.0

B   + 0.4

C   − 0.6

D   − 1.0

166 Regression analysis is being used to find the line of best fit (y = a + bx) from five pairs of data. The calculations have produced the following information:

$\Sigma x = 129$ $\Sigma y = 890$ $\Sigma xy = 23{,}091$ $\Sigma x^2 = 3{,}433$ $\Sigma y^2 = 29{,}929$

What is the value of 'a' in the equation for the line of best fit (to the nearest whole number)?

A   146

B   152

C   210

D   245

167 Which of the following is a feasible value for a correlation coefficient?

A   +1.2

B   0

C   −1.2

D   −2.0

168 Put the stages of the product life cycle in the correct order:

(i)   Growth

(ii)   Decline

(iii)   Maturity

(iv)   Development

(v)   Introduction

A   (i), (v), (iii), (iv), (ii)

B   (v), (iv), (i), (iii), (ii)

C   (iv), (v), (i), (iii), (ii)

D   (iv), (i), (iv), (iii), (ii)

169 An inflation index and index numbers of a company's sales (€) for the last year are given below.

Quarter:	1	2	3	4
Sales (€) index:	109	120	132	145
Inflation index:	100	110	121	133

'Real' sales, i.e. adjusted for inflation, are:

A   approximately constant and keeping up with inflation

B   growing steadily and not keeping up with inflation

C   growing steadily and keeping ahead of inflation

D   falling steadily and not keeping up with inflation

170 Four years ago material X cost $5 per kg and the price index most appropriate to the cost of material X stood at 150. The same index now stands at 430.

What is the best estimate of the current cost of material X per kg?

A $1.74

B $9.33

C $14.33

D $21.50

The following data are to be used for questions 171 and 172

The managers of the catering division of a hospital wish to develop an index number series for measuring changes in food prices. As an experiment, they have chosen four items in general use which are summarised below:

	Prices per unit		Quantities	
	20X1	20X2	20X1	20X2
Flour (kgs)	0.25	0.30	8,000	10,000
Eggs (boxes)	1.00	1.25	4,000	5,000
Milk (litres)	0.30	0.35	10,000	10,000
Potatoes (kgs)	0.05	0.06	6,000	10,000

---

171 Based on 20X1 as 100, calculate the Paasche price index for 20X2.

A 82.4

B 121.36

C 121.08

D 82.6

172 Based on 20X1 as 100, calculate the Laspeyres price index for 20X2.

A 82.4

B 121.36

C 121.08

D 82.6

The following data are to be used for questions 173 and 174

A company is preparing its forecast sales information for the end of the current year. The actual sales information for the first nine months of the current year (20X1) is below:

	Sales volume (units)
January	172,100
February	149,600
March	165,800
April	182,600
May	160,100
June	197,100
July	174,600
August	190,800
September	207,600

173 The sales volume trend is to be identified using a 5-point moving average.

What is the monthly trend?

A   50 units

B   500 units

C   5,000 units

D   50,000 units

174 What is the expected sales volume including seasonal variation for December 20X1

A   206,040 units

B   211,040 units

C   222,480 units

D   199,600 units

175 Which of the following are components of a time series analysis?

(i)   Trend

(ii)   Seasonal variation

(iii) Cyclical variation

A   (i) and (ii) only

B   (i) and (iii) only

C   (ii) and (iii) only

D   (i), (ii) and (iii)

176 Two years ago the price index appropriate to the cost of material X had a value of 120. It now has a value of 160.

If material X costs $2,000 per kg today, what would its cost per kg have been two years ago?

A $1,500

B $1,667

C $2,667

D $3,200

177 A time series model of sales volume has the following trend and additive seasonal variation.

Trend

Y = 5,000 + 4,000 X.

Where Y = quarterly sales volume in units.

X = the quarter number (Where the first quarter of 2009 = quarter 17, the second quarter of 2009 = quarter 18 etc).

Seasonal variation

Quarter	Seasonal variation (units)
First	+3,000
Second	+1,000
Third	−1,500
Fourth	−2,500

What would be the time series forecast of sales units for the third quarter of 2010?

- A   79,500
- B   95,500
- C   97,000
- D   98,500

The following data are to be used for questions 178 and 179

A company is preparing its annual budget and is estimating the cost of production. The company has the identified the following trend for the production of its product:

y = a + bx where

y = number of units produced in a month

a = 3,000 units

b = 150 units

x = the month number (January 20X1 is month 1, February 20X1 is month 2, etc).

For the first 6 months of 20X1 the actual production, which was affected by seasonal variations, was as follows:

	Units produced
January	3,000
February	3,250
March	3,500
April	3,750
May	3,825
June	3,825

---

178   **Calculate the seasonal variation for March 20X1**

- A   +50
- B   -50
- C   +75
- D   -75

179   **Calculate the expected production for March 20X2 after adjusting for the seasonal variation using the additive model**

- A   5,250 units
- B   5,200 units
- C   5,300 units
- D   5,150 units

180　The product life cycle model has 5 stages – for how many of the stages is it thought that a loss could be made?

 A 1

 B 2

 C 3

 D 4

The following data are to be used for questions 181 and 182

A company buys and uses five different materials. Details of the actual prices and quantities used for 20X1 and the budgeted figures for 20X2 are as follows:

	Actual 20X1		Budgeted 20X2	
Material	Quantity (000)	Unit price $	Quantity (000)	Unit price $
F	21	11	25	12
G	56	22	52	26
H	62	18	79	18
I	29	20	35	22
J	31	22	36	23

181　Calculate a Laspeyre price index for material prices based on 20X1 = 100.

 A 108.7

 B 92.0

 C 107.8

 D 92.7

182　Calculate a Paasche price index for material prices based on 20X1 = 100.

 A 108.7

 B 92.0

 C 107.8

 D 92.7

BUDGETING

183　The main purposes of budgeting are:

 (i) to give authority to spend

 (ii) to control expenditure

 (iii) to aid decision making.

 A (i) only

 B (i) and (ii) only

 C (ii) only

 D (i), (ii) and (iii)

184 The budget committee is made up of representatives from the finance function and co-ordinates the budget planning process.

This statement is:

A True

B False

185 A business is preparing its production budget for the year ahead for product A998. It is estimated that 100,000 units of A998 can be sold in the year and the opening inventory is currently 14,000 units. The inventory level is to be reduced by 40% by the end of the year.

The number of units of A998 needed to be produced is:

A 86,000

B 94,400

C 100,000

D 108,400

186 The production budget is calculated by taking the sales budget adding the opening inventory of finished goods and subtracting the closing inventory of finished goods.

This statement is:

A True

B False

187 A process has a normal loss of 10% and budgeted output is 4,500 litres for the period. Opening inventory of raw material is 600 litres and is expected to increase by 20% by the end of the period.

The material usage budget is:

A 4,500 litres

B 5,000 litres

C 5,133 litres

D 5,120 litres

188 The material usage budget is calculated by taking the production budget and multiplying by the standard material quantity per unit.

This statement is:

A True

B False

189 A company has a budget for two products A and B as follows:

	Product A	Product B
Sales (units)	2,000	4,500
Production (units)	1,750	5,000

Labour:		
Skilled at $10/hour	2 hours/unit	2 hours/unit
Unskilled at $7/hour	3 hours/unit	4 hours/unit

What is the budgeted cost for unskilled labour for the period?

A $105,000

B $135,000

C $176,750

D $252,500

190 The principal budget factor for a footwear retailer is:

A   The cost item taking the largest share of total expenditure.

B   The product line contributing the largest amount to sales revenue.

C   The product line contributing the largest amount to business profits.

D   The constraint that is expected to limit the retailer's activities during the budget period.

191 A company makes 2 products, X and Y, which are sold in the ratio 1:2. The selling prices are $50 and $100 respectively. The company wants to earn $100,000 over the next period. The sales budget should be:

	X (units)	Y (units)
A	1,334	667
B	800	400
C	667	1,334
D	400	800

192 A budget manual will include which of the following?

(i)   An organisation chart

(ii)   A budget timetable

(iii)   Copies of budget forms

(iv)   Key assumptions to be used in the budget

A   (ii), (iii) and (iv)

B   (ii) and (iv)

C   (iii) and (iv)

D   all of these

193 A business is preparing its production budget, materials usage and materials purchases budget for the forthcoming period. The following information is known:

Budgeted sales	2,300 units
Current inventory of finished goods	400 units
Required closing inventory of finished goods	550 units

Each unit of the product uses 6 kg of material X and details of this are as follows:

Current inventory of X	2,000 kg
Required closing inventory of X	2,600 kg

The amount of production volume required for the forthcoming period to meet the sales demand is:

A   3,050 units

B   2,450 units

C   2,300 units

D   2,150 units

194   A company makes three products, X, Y and Z. The following information is available:

	X	Y	Z
Budgeted production (units)	200	400	300
Machine hours per unit	5	6	2

Variable overheads	$2.30 per machine hour
Fixed overheads	$0.75 per machine hour

The overhead budget is:

A $12,200

B $12,000

C $11,590

D $10,980

The following information should be used for questions 195, 196 and 197

A toy manufacturer produces two products, a clockwork clown and a wind-up train. Standard cost data for the products are as follows:

	Clockwork clown	Wind-up train
Direct materials ($5 per kg)	2 kg	1 kg
Direct labour ($8 per hour)	18 minutes	30 minutes
Budgeted sales	450	550
Budgeted inventories are as follows:		
Finished goods		
Opening inventory	20	50
Closing inventory	30	40
Raw materials		
Opening inventory	50 kg	
Closing inventory	60 kg	

---

195   The total direct material usage budget is:

A   1,540 kg

B   1,470 kg

C   1,460 kg

D   1,440 kg

196 **The total direct material purchases budget is:**

A $7,350

B $7,300

C $7,250

D $7,200

197 **The total direct labour budget is:**

A $3,264

B $3,280

C $3,290

D $3,296

198 **A job requires 2,400 actual labour hours for completion but it is anticipated that idle time will be 20% of the total time required. If the wage rate is $10 per hour, what is the budgeted labour cost for the job, including the cost of the idle time?**

A $19,200

B $24,000

C $28,800

D $30,000

199 **Which of the following statements about imposed budgets are correct?**

(i)   Imposed budgets are likely to set realistic targets because senior management have the best idea of what is achievable in each part of the business.

(ii)   Imposed budgets can be less effective than budgets set on a participative basis, because it is difficult for an individual to be motivated to achieve targets set by someone else.

(iii)   Imposed budgets are generally quicker to prepare and finalise than participative budgets.

A   (i) and (ii) only

B   (i) and (iii) only

C   (ii) and (iii) only

D   (iii) only

CAPITAL BUDGETING

200 **The details of an investment project are as follows:**

Cost of asset bought at the start of the project	$80,000
Annual cash inflow	$25,000
Cost of capital	5% each year
Life of the project	8 years

The present value of the project is:

A   -$120,000

B $120,000

C $81,575

D   -$81,575

201 A company is planning to open a new store in a new geographic location. An initial site evaluation has taken place at a cost of $5,000 and a store location has been found. The new store can be rented for $9,500 per annum. It will require refurbishment at a cost of $320,000.

Which of the following costs are relevant for an NPV calculation?

(i) $5,000

(ii) $9,500

(iii) $320,000

A   (i) only

B   (i) and (ii)

C   (ii) and (iii)

D   (iii) only

202 B Company is deciding whether to launch a new product. The initial outlay for the product is $60,000. The forecast possible annual cash inflows and their associated probabilities are shown below:

Year 0	(60,000)
Year 1	23,350
Year 2	29,100
Year 3	27,800

The company's cost of capital is 8% per annum.

Assume the cash inflows are received at the end of the year and that the cash inflows for each year are independent.

The expected net present value for the product is:

A   ($500)

B $8,634

C $10,189

D $12,348

203 An education authority is considering the implementation of a CCTV (closed circuit television) security system in one of its schools. Details of the proposed project are as follows:

Life of project	5 years
Initial cost	$75,000
Annual savings:	
Labour costs	$20,000
Other costs	$5,000
NPV at 15%	$8,800

Calculate the internal rate of return for this project to the nearest 1%

A   16%

B   18%

C   20%

D   22%

204 The following measures have been calculated to appraise a proposed project

The internal rate of return is 12%

The return on capital employed is 16%

The payback period is 4 years

Which of the following statements is correct?

A   the payback is less than 5 years so the project should go ahead

B   the IRR is lower than the return on capital employed so the project should not go ahead

C   the IRR is greater than the cost of capital so the project should go ahead

D   The IRR is positive so the project should go ahead

205 CC Company is considering an investment of $300,000 which will earn a contribution of $40,000 each year for 10 years at today's prices. The company's cost of capital is 11% per annum.

Calculate the net present value of the project.

A   ($64,440)

B $23,556

C $64,440

D $235,560

206 Sandwich Queen is looking to expand its restaurant facilities to increase its seating capacity a further 40%. Results for the current year are:

	$000	$000
Food sales	200	
Drink sales	170	
		370
Food costs	145	
Drink costs	77	
Staff costs	40	
Other costs	20	
		282
Cash flow		88

Sales and variable costs will increase in line with the seating capacity increase. The other costs are 40% fixed. An extra employee will be required to serve the extra seating capacity. There are currently 4 employees on an equal wage.

What is the relevant annual net cash flow of the proposed expansion?

A   Nil

B $41,000

C $44,000

D $47,000

207 JAH Company is about to invest $400,000 in machinery and other capital equipment for a new product venture. Cash flows for the first three years are estimated as follows

Year	$000
1	210
2	240
3	320

JAH Company requires a 17% return for projects of this type. What is the NPV of this venture?

A   -$154,670

B $45,010

C $220,450

D $154,670

208 A company has determined that the net present value of an investment project is $17,706 when using a 10% discount rate and $(4,317) when using a discount rate of 15%.

Calculate the internal rate of return of the project to the nearest 1%.

A   13%

B   14%

C   15%

D   16%

209 A company is considering an investment of $400,000 in new machinery. The machinery is expected to yield incremental profits over the next five years as follows:

Year	Profit ($)
1	175,000
2	225,000
3	340,000
4	165,000
5	125,000

Thereafter, no incremental profits are expected and the machinery will be sold. It is company policy to depreciate machinery on a straight line basis over the life of the asset. The machinery is expected to have a value of $50,000 at the end of year 5.

Calculate the payback period of the investment in this machinery to the nearest 0.1 years.

A   0.9 years

B   1.3 years

C   1.5 years

D   1.9 years

210 An interest rate that includes the effect of compounding is known as:

A   Nominal interest

B   Simple interest

C   Compound interest

D   Effective interest

211   Which of the following statements are true about IRRs?

(i)   IRR considers the time value of money

(ii)   if the IRR exceeds the companies cost of capital the NPV at the company's cost of capital should be positive

(iii)   it is possible for one investment to have 2 IRRs

A   (i) only

B   (i) and (ii) only

C   (ii) and (iii) only

D   (i), (ii) and (iii)

BUDGETARY CONTROL

212   A flexible budget is

A   a budget for semi-variable overhead costs only;

B   a budget which, by recognising different cost behaviour patterns, is designed to change as volume of activity changes;

C   a budget for a twelve month period which includes planned revenues, expenses, assets and liabilities;

D   a budget which is prepared for a rolling period which is reviewed monthly, and updated accordingly.

213   A purpose of a flexible budget is:

A   to cap discretionary expenditure

B   to produce a revised forecast by changing the original budget when actual costs are known

C   to control resource efficiency

D   to communicate target activity levels within an organisation by setting a budget in advance of the period to which it relates.

214   A fixed budget is:

A   a budget for a single level of activity

B   used when the mix of products is fixed in advance of the budget period

C   a budget which ignores inflation

D   an overhead cost budget.

215 Which of the following statements are correct?

(i)   A fixed budget is a budget that considers all of an organisation's costs and revenues for a single level of activity.

(ii) A flexible budget is a budget that is produced during the budget period to recognise the effects of any changes in prices and methods of operation that have occurred.

(iii) Organisations can use budgets to communicate objectives to their managers.

A   (i) and (ii) only

B   (i) and (iii) only

C   (ii) and (iii) only

D   All of them

216 The volume variance is the difference between the flexible budget and the actual results.

This statement is:

A   True

B   False

The following information should be used for questions 217 and 218

Oswald Press produces and sells textbooks for schools and colleges. The following budgeted information is available for the year ending 31 December 20X6:

	Budget	Actual
Sales (units)	120,000	100,000
	$000	$000
Sales revenue	1,200	995
Variable printing costs	360	280
Variable production overheads	60	56
Fixed production cost	300	290
Fixed administration cost	360	364
Profit	120	5

---

217 The flexed budget shows:

A   a profit of $10,000

B   a loss of $10,000

C   a profit of $100,000

D   a loss of $100,000

218 The total expenditure and volume variances are:

	Expenditure variance	Volume variance
A	$15,000 favourable	$130,000 adverse
B	$95,000 adverse	$115,000 favourable
C	$115,000 adverse	$95,000 favourable
D	$130,000 adverse	$15,000 favourable

219 **In a responsibility accounting system which of the following costs is least likely to appear on the performance report for the foreman of a production department?**

A   Cost of direct labour

B   Rent of machinery

C   Repairs to machinery

D   Cost of materials used

220 **In a responsibility accounting system for which of the following should the production line manager be held responsible?**

A   Raw material prices and labour wage rates

B   Raw material usage and labour wage rates

C   Raw material prices and labour hours worked

D   Raw material usage and labour hours worked

STANDARD COSTING

221 **Which of the following techniques would be useful for controlling costs?**

(i)   Actual versus flexed budget

(ii)   Variance analysis

(iii)   Trend of costs analysis

A   (i) and (ii) only

B   (i) and (iii) only

C   (ii) and (iii) only

D   (i), (ii) and (iii)

222 **When considering setting standards for costing which of the following would NOT be appropriate?**

A   The normal level of activity should always be used for absorbing overheads.

B   Average prices for materials should be used, encompassing any discounts that are regularly available.

C   The labour rate used will be the rate at which labour is paid.

D   Average material usage should be established based on generally-accepted working practices.

223 **A company uses standard marginal costing. Last month the standard contribution on actual sales was $10,000 and the following variances arose :**

Total variable costs variance	$2,000 adverse
Sales Price variance	$500 favourable
Sales volume contribution variance	$1,000 adverse

What was the actual contribution for last month?

A $7,000

B $7,500

C $8,000

D $8,500

224 A company uses standard marginal costing. Last month, when all sales were at the standard selling price, the standard contribution from actual sales was $50,000 and the following variances arose :

Total variable cost variance	$3,500 Adverse
Total fixed costs variance	$1,000 favourable
Sales volume contribution variance	$2,000 favourable

What was the actual contribution for last month?

A $46,500

B $47,500

C $48,500

D $49,500

225 The following information relates to labour costs for the past month:

Budget	Labour rate	$10 per hour
	Production time	15,000 hours
	Time per unit	3 hours
	Production units	5,000 units
Actual	Wages paid	$176,000
	Production	5,500 units
	Total hours worked	14,000 hours

There was no idle time.

What were the labour rate and efficiency variances?

	Rate variance	Efficiency variance
A	$26,000 adverse	$25,000 favourable
B	$26,000 adverse	$10,000 favourable
C	$36,000 adverse	$2,500 favourable
D	$36,000 adverse	$25,000 favourable

226 The following details relate to product T, which has a selling price of $44.00:

	$/unit
Direct materials	15.00
Direct labour (3 hours)	12.00
Variable overhead	6.00
Fixed overhead	4.00
	37.00

During April 20X6, the actual production of T was 800 units, which was 100 units fewer than budgeted. The budget shows an annual production target of 10,800, with fixed costs accruing at a constant rate throughout the year. Actual overhead expenditure totalled $8,500 for April 20X6.

Overheads are absorbed on the basis of units produced.

The overhead variances for April 20X6 were:

	Expenditure $	Volume $
A	367 A	1,000 A
B	500 A	400 A
C	100 A	1,000 A
D	100 A	400 A

227 A company operates a standard marginal costing system. Last month its actual fixed overhead expenditure was 10% above budget resulting in a fixed overhead expenditure variance of $36,000.

What was the actual expenditure on fixed overheads last month?

A $324,000

B $360,000

C $396,000

D $400,000

228 FGH has the following budgeted and actual data:

Budgeted fixed overhead cost	$120,000
Budgeted production (units)	20,000
Actual fixed overhead cost	$115,000
Actual production (units)	21,000

The fixed overhead volume variance:

A is $4,500 adverse

B is $5,500 favourable

C is $6,000 favourable

D is $10,500 favourable

229 A company budgeted to make 30,000 units of a product P. Each unit was expected to take 4 hours to make and budgeted fixed overhead expenditure was $840,000. Actual production of product P in the period was 32,000 units, which took 123,000 hours to make. Actual fixed overhead expenditure was $885,600.

What was the fixed overhead capacity variance for the period?

A $21,000 favourable

B $21,000 adverse

C $35,000 adverse

D $56,000 favourable

230 QRL uses a standard absorption costing system. The following details have been extracted from its budget for April 20X7:

Fixed production overhead cost	$48,000
Production (units)	4,800

In April 20X7 the fixed production overhead cost was under-absorbed by $8,000 and the fixed production overhead expenditure variance was $2,000 adverse.

The actual number of units produced was:

A   3,800

B   4,000

C   4,200

D   5,400

231   **Performance standards that have remained unchanged over a long period of time are known as:**

A   ideal standards

B   current standards

C   basic standards

D   attainable standards.

232   **Standard costing may be inappropriate in the modern business environment because quality is now as important, if not more, than price.**

This statement is:

A   True

B   False

233   **A company has a higher than expected staff turnover and as a result staff are less experienced than expected.**

As an indirect result of this, are the labour rate variance and material usage variance likely to be adverse or favourable?

	Labour rate	Material usage
A	Favourable	Favourable
B	Adverse	Favourable
C	Favourable	Adverse
D	Adverse	Adverse

234   **A company is obliged to buy sub-standard materials at lower than standard price because nothing else is available.**

As an indirect result of this purchase, are the materials usage variance and labour efficiency variance likely to be adverse or favourable?

	Materials usage	Labour efficiency
A	Favourable	Favourable
B	Adverse	Favourable
C	Favourable	Adverse
D	Adverse	Adverse

235   **Fawley's direct labour cost data relating to last month were as follows:**

Standard labour cost of actual hours worked	$116,000
Standard hours worked	30,000
Standard rate per hour	$4
Labour rate variance	$5,800 favourable
Labour efficiency variance	$4,000 favourable

The actual rate of pay per hour was:

A $3.80

B $3.81

C $3.94

D $3.99

236   Michel has the following results.

10,080 hours actually worked and paid costing $8,770

If the rate variance is $706 adverse, the efficiency variance $256 favourable, and 5,000 units were produced, what is the standard production time per unit?

A   1.95 hours

B   1.96 hours

C   2.07 hours

D   2.08 hours

237   An extract from the standard cost card for product CJ is as follows:

Direct labour (0.5 hours × $12) $6

710 units of CJ were produced in the period and staff worked 378 hours at a total cost of $4,725. Of these hours 20 were lost due to a material shortage.

The labour efficiency variance is:

A $516 favourable

B $36 favourable

C $36 adverse

D $516 adverse

38   A company makes a single product. The following details are from the cost card for the product:

Direct labour	10 hours at $5 per hour
Variable overhead	10 hours at $1.50 per hour

The actual results for the last period are:

500 units produced

Labour	4,800 hours
Variable overheads	$7,700

The variable overhead expenditure and efficiency variances are:

	Expenditure	Efficiency
A	$300 A	$500 F
B	$300 F	$500 A
C	$500 A	$300 F
D	$500 F	$300 A

239 A company uses standard absorption costing. The following data relate to last month:

	Budget	Actual
Sales and production (units)	1,000	900

	Standard $	Actual $
Selling price per unit	50	52
Total production cost per unit	39	40

What was the adverse sales volume profit variance last month?

A $1,000

B $1,100

C $1,200

D $1,300

240 A company operates a standard marginal costing system. Last month actual fixed overhead expenditure was 2% below budget and the fixed overhead expenditure variance was $1,250.

What was the actual fixed overhead expenditure for last month?

A $61,250

B $62,475

C $62,500

D $63,750

241 Under absorption costing principles a favourable sales volume variance is calculated as the difference in sales volumes multiplied by :

A Standard contribution per unit

B Standard cost per unit

C Standard profit per unit

D Standard selling price per unit

242 The sales volume variance will be the same whether marginal or absorption costing is used.

This statement is:

A True

B False

The following information relates to questions 243 and 244

The standard direct material cost for a product is $50 per unit (12.5 kg at $4 per kg). Last month the actual amount paid for 45,600 kg of material purchased and used was $173,280 and the direct material usage variance was $15,200 adverse.

---

243 What was the direct material price variance last month?

A $8,800 adverse

B $8,800 favourable

C $9,120 adverse

D $9,120 favourable

244   What was the actual production last month?

A   3,344 units

B   3,520 units

C   3,952 units

D   4,160 units

245   A new machine is purchased which is more expensive, but requires less labour to operate per unit.

The impact on the fixed overhead variances will be:

	Expenditure variance	Volume variance
A	Adverse	Adverse
B	Adverse	Favourable
C	Favourable	Favourable
D	Favourable	Favourable

246   QR has budgeted to produce 4,000 units in January. Actual production was 3,700 units with fixed production overheads of $10,300. The standard fixed overhead cost per unit was 1.5 hours at $2.40 per hour. 5,800 actual production hours were worked.

What was the fixed overhead volume variance?

A $1,080 favourable

B $480 favourable

C $480 adverse

D $1,080 adverse

247   Which of the following could be the cause of an adverse sales volume variance for garden furniture.

(i)   The company offers discounts on sales prices in order to maintain business.

(ii)   Poor weather leads to a reduction in sales.

(iii)   A strike in the factory causes a shortage of finished goods.

A   (i) and (ii) only

B   (i) and (iii) only

C   (ii) and (iii) only

248 The following information relates to April production of product CK:

	Actual	Budget
Units produced	580	600
Input of material (kg)	1,566	1,500
Cost of material purchased and input	$77,517	$76,500

What is the materials usage variance?

A $2,349 favourable

B $3,366 adverse

C $5,742 adverse

D $5,916 adverse

249 For product DR, the material price variance for the month of August was $1,000 (Favourable) and the material usage variance was $300 (Adverse).

The standard material usage per unit is 3 kg, and the standard material price is $2 per kg. 500 units were produced in the period. Opening inventories of raw materials were 100 kg and closing inventories 400 kg.

Material purchases in the period were:

A 1,050 kg

B 1,350 kg

C 1,650 kg

D 1,950 kg

250 The following information relates to a month's production of product CN:

	Budget	Actual
Units produced	600	580
Input of material P (kg)	1,500	1,566
Cost of material P purchased and input	$25,500	$25,839

What is the price variance for material P?

A $783 favourable

B $339 adverse

C $1,189 adverse

D $1,972 adverse

251 A company uses a standard absorption costing system. Last month budgeted production was 8,000 units and the standard fixed production overhead cost was $15 per unit. Actual production last month was 8,500 units and the actual fixed production overhead cost was $17 per unit.

What was the total adverse fixed production overhead variance for last month?

A $7,500

B $16,000

C $17,000

D $24,500

(2 marks)

252 A company is reviewing actual performance to budget to see where there are differences. The following standard information is relevant:

	$ per unit
Selling price	50
	—
Direct materials	4
Direct labour	16
Fixed production overheads	5
Variable production overheads	10
Fixed selling costs	1
Variable selling cost	1
	—
Total costs	37
	—
Budgeted sales units	3,000
Actual sales units	3,500

What was the favourable sales volume variance using marginal costing?

A $9,500

B $7,500

C $7,000

D $6,500

253 A company uses variance analysis to control costs and revenues.

Information concerning sales is as follows:

Budgeted selling price	$15 per unit
Budgeted sales units	10,000
Budgeted profit per unit	$5
Actual sales revenue	$151,500
Actual units sold	9,800

What is the sales volume profit variance?

A $500 favourable

B $1,000 favourable

C $1,000 adverse

D $3,000 adverse

254 A company operates a standard absorption costing system. The standard fixed production overhead rate is $15 per hour.

The following data relate to last month:

Actual hours worked	5,500
Budgeted hours	5,000
Standard hours for actual production	4,800

What was the fixed production overhead capacity variance?

A $7,500 adverse

B $7,500 favourable

C $10,500 adverse

D $10,500 favourable

255 Direct labour cost data relating to last month is as follows:

Actual hours worked	28,000
Total direct labour cost	$117,600
Direct labour rate variance	$8,400 adverse
Direct labour efficiency variance	$3,900 favourable

To the nearest thousand hours, what were the standard labour hours for actual production last month?

A 31,000 hrs

B 29,000 hrs

C 27,000 hrs

D 25,000 hrs

PERFORMANCE MEASUREMENT TECHNIQUES

256 In the last year a division's controllable return on investment was 25% and its controllable profit was $80,000. The cost of finance appropriate to the division was 18% per annum.

What was the division's controllable residual income in the last year?

A $5,600

B $22,400

C $74,400

D $76,400

257 A government body uses measures based upon the 'three Es' to the measure value for money generated by a publicly funded hospital. It considers the most important performance measure to be 'cost per successfully treated patient'.

Which of the three E's best describes the above measure?

A Economy

B Effectiveness

C Efficiency

D Externality

258 Which of the following are elements of a mission statement?

(i) Purpose

(ii) Strategy

(iii) Values

(iv) Culture

A   All of them

B   (i) and (ii) only

C   (ii) only

D   (ii) and (iv) only

259   A government is looking at assessing hospitals by reference to a range of both financial and non-financial factors, one of which is survival rates for heart by-pass operation.

Which of the three E's best describes the above measure?

A   Economy

B   Effectiveness

C   Efficiency

D   Externality

260   Which of the following measures would not be appropriate for a cost centre?

A   Cost per unit

B   Contribution per unit

C   Comparison of actual labour cost to budget labour cost

D   Under or over absorption of overheads

261   A government is looking at assessing state schools by reference to a range of both financial and non-financial factors, one of which is average class sizes.

Which of the three E's best describes the above measure?

A   Economy

B   Effectiveness

C   Efficiency

D   Externality

262   Copenhagen is an insurance company. Recently there has been concern that too many quotations have been sent to clients either late or containing errors.

The department concerned has responded that it is understaffed, and a high proportion of current staff has recently joined the firm. The performance of this department is to be carefully monitored.

Which ONE of the following non-financial performance indicators would NOT be an appropriate measure to monitor and improve the department's performance?

A   Percentage of quotations found to contain errors when checked

B   Percentage of quotations not issued within company policy of three working days

C   Percentage of department's quota of staff actually employed

D   Percentage of budgeted number of quotations actually issued

263 For operational purposes, for a company operating a fleet of delivery vehicles, which of the following would be most useful?

A   Cost per mile run

B   Cost per driver hour

C   Cost per tonne mile

D   Cost per kg carried

264 A division has a residual income of £240,000 and a net profit before imputed interest of £640,000.

If it uses a rate of 10% for computing imputed interest on its invested capital, what is its return on investment (ROI) to the nearest whole number?

A   4%

B   10%

C   16%

D   27%

265 An organisation is divided into a number of divisions, each of which operates as a profit centre. Which of the following would be useful measures to monitor divisional performance?

(i)   Contribution

(ii)   Controllable profit

(iii) Return on investment

(iv)   Residual income

A   (i) only

B   (i) and (ii) only

C   (iii) and (iv) only

D   All of them

266 JKL Inc budgeted to make 1,000 units in May using 2,000 hours of direct labour. Actual output was 1,100 units which took 2,300 hours.

Calculate the production/volume ratio.

A   91%

B   105%

C   110%

D   115%

267 RL Inc budgeted to make 200 units in June with a standard labour usage of 0.6 hours per unit. Actual output was 180 units which took 126 hours.

Calculate the efficiency ratio.

A   86%

B   90%

C   105%

D   116%

268   CAP Inc budgeted to make 50 units in July with a standard labour usage of 1.2 hours per unit. Actual output was 49 units which took 61 hours.

Calculate the capacity ratio.

A   96%

B   98%

C   100%

D   102%

269   HH plc monitors the % of total sales that derives from products developed in the last year. Which part of the balanced scorecard would this measure be classified under?

A   Financial perspective

B   Customer perspective

C   Internal perspective

D   Learning perspective

270   Which of the following KPIs would be used to assess the liquidity of a company?

(i)   Return on capital employed

(ii)   Gross profit percentage

(iii) Acid test ratio

(iv)   Gearing ratio

A   (i) and (ii) only

B   (iii) only

C   (iv) only

D   (iii) and (iv) only

271   A company wants to encourage an investment centre to make new investments. Performance measurement using which of the following KPIs would achieve this?

A   ROI

B   ROCE

C   RI

D   IRR

272   Why would a company want to encourage the use of non-financial performance indicators?

A   To encourage short termism

B   To look at the fuller picture of the business

C   To enable results to be easily manipulated to the benefit of the manager

D   To prevent goal congruence

273 K Class has calculated the following indictors

(i)   Return on capital employed

(ii)   Training costs as a percentage of total costs

Which of the balanced scorecard perspectives would these measures relate to?

	(i)	(ii)
A	Financial	Financial
B	Financial	Internal
C	Internal	Learning and growth
D	Financial	Learning and growth

274 Area 27 are a pizza delivery company and have asked you to suggest some performance indicators that could be used to measure the customer perspective and the internal perspective of the balanced scorecard. Which of the following would be appropriate?

	Customer	Internal
A	Number of customer complaints	Time taken from order to delivery pizza
B	Cost per pizza	Cost of time spent on training
C	Number of late deliveries	Profit per pizza
D	Cost of delivery vehicles	Gross profit percentage

275 Which of the following is not a type of benchmarking?

A   Internal

B   Strategic

C   International

D   Functional

SPREADSHEETS

276 The following statements relate to spreadsheets:

(i)   A spreadsheet consists of records and files.

(ii)   Most spreadsheets have a facility to allow data within them to be displayed graphically.

(iii)   A spreadsheet could be used to prepare a budgeted income statement.

(iv)   A spreadsheet is the most suitable software for storing large volumes of data.

Which of the above statements are correct?

A   (i) and (ii) only

B   (i), (iii) and (iv) only

C   (ii) and (iii) only

D   (iii) and (iv) only

277 John has produced the following spreadsheet to calculate the correlation coefficient between average daily fruit and vegetable intake (measured in normal portions) and success in exams (number of passes above C grade).

	A	B	C	D	E	F
1	Correlation					
2		Vitamins	Exam			
3		x	y	xy	x^2	y^2
4		0	6			
5		1	5			
6		2	4			
7		3	4			
8		4	6			
9		5	7			
10		6	7			
11	Totals					
12						
13	Correlation coefficient		=			
14						
15						

What should the formula in cell D13 be?

A   (6*D11-B11*C11)/((6*E11-B11^2)*(6*F11-C11^2))^0.5

B   (7*D11-B11*C11)/((7*E11-B11^2)*(7*F11-C11^2))

C   (7*D11-B11*C11)/((7*E11-B11^2)*(7*F11-C11^2))^0.5

D   (6*D11-B11*C11)/((6*E11-B11^2)*(6*F11-C11^2))

278 Which of the following are advantages of spreadsheet software over manual approaches?

(i)   Security

(ii)   Speed

(iii)   Accuracy

(iv)   Legibility

A   All of them

B   (ii), (iii) and (iv)

C   (ii) and (iv)

D   (i) and (iv)

279 A company manufactures a single product. In a computer spreadsheet the cells F1 to F12 contain the budgeted monthly sales units for the 12 months of next year in sequence with January sales in cell F1 and finishing with December sales in F12. The company policy is for the closing inventory of finished goods each month to be 10% of the budgeted sales units for the following month.

Which of the following formulae will generate the budgeted production (in units) for March next year?

A   =[F3 +(0.1*F4)]

B   =[F3 -(0.1*F4)]

C   =[(1.1*F3) - (0.1*F4)]

D   =[(0.9*F3) +(0.1*F4)]

280 Which of the following is not one of the main aspects of formatting cells?

A   Wrapping text

B   Using graphics

C   Setting number specification, e.g. working to 2 decimal places

D   Changing the font, size or colour of text

Section 2

ANSWERS TO PRACTICE QUESTIONS

THE NATURE AND PURPOSE OF MANAGEMENT ACCOUNTING

1   **D**

2   **A**

Reginald is only responsible for costs

3   **A**

Cost accounting can be used for inventory valuation to meet the requirements of both internal reporting and external financial reporting.

4   **B**

Cost accounting is not part of financial accounting.

5   **A**

Qualitative data is normally non-numerical. Information comes from both internal and external sources. Operational information is usually short-term (current) in nature.

6   **C**

The manager of a profit centre needs to know about the profits of the centre, i.e. revenues and costs. (Revenues only are appropriate for a revenue centre; costs only for a cost centre; and revenues, costs and assets employed for an investment centre.)

7   **C**

Lowering a selling price, presumably to increase sales volume, is a short-term decision/plan. The measures in A, B and D are not planning decisions at all: they are all monitoring/control activities.

8   **B**

Strategic planning is carried out by senior managers and is concerned with long-term planning. Both quantitative and qualitative information is used.

9   C

    (i)   ROCE compares profit to capital employed and is not a suitable measure for a profit centre as the manager does not have responsibility for capital employed.

    (ii)   Cost centres are found in all organisations.

    (iii)   The manager of a revenue centre is only responsible for revenues, not costs.

10   A

The mixing and pouring departments are cost centres. The paint is not poured into tins until after the colour adding department so a litre tin would not be a suitable cost unit.

SOURCES OF DATA

11   B

The information should be sufficiently accurate given time and cost constraints. Managers should be made aware of the degree of accuracy of the information.

12   C

13   C

This is the definition of systematic sampling.

14   B

Simple random sampling always eliminates selection bias but does not guarantee a representative sample.

15   D

Accountant first stratifies the invoices according to value and then selects randomly. Sampling method is stratified.

16   D

Option A is not random – it is a stratified sample.

Option B selects only those who are in a class – so it is NOT random.

Option C, again, is not random as it only selects from 10% of colleges (and therefore does not include home study, or the other 90%).

PRESENTING INFORMATION

17   D

A simple bar chart would show five bars illustrating the different salaries in different regions.

18 C

The sales revenue is dependent on the money spent on advertising. The more advertising that is done the higher the sales revenue should be. Not vice versa

19 A

360/1384 × 241 = 62.69°

20 B

45°/360° × $800,000 = $100,000

TYPES OF COST AND COST BEHAVIOUR

21 D

Options B and C would begin from 0 and are clearly incorrect. Option A would be similar to the graph given except it would be flat at the top due to the maximum annual charge.

22 A

Variable cost per unit = [($274,000 – $250,000) ÷ (15,000 – 12,000)] = $8

Total fixed cost above 11,000 units = [$274,000 – (15,000 × $8)] = $154,000

Total fixed cost below 11,000 units = (10 ÷ 11) × $154,000 = $140,000

Total cost for 10,000 units = [(10,000 × $8) + $140,000] = $220,000

23 B

As the royalty relates to every unit produced, it is therefore classified as a direct expense.

24 B

Inventory is valued at full production cost.

25 A

Supervisor's wages are usually classified as a step cost because a supervisor may be responsible for supervising up to a specific number of workers. However, if output increases such that additional direct labour is required, then an extra supervisor will be required.

     1 – 10 workers   1 supervisor

     11 – 20 workers   2 supervisors

26 C

C is the correct answer because a manager is not a cost object but may be linked to a cost centre in a responsibility accounting system.

27 B

Answers A and C are both incorrect, leaving B as the only possible answer. Depreciation of fixtures is an overhead cost, and could be production, administration or selling and distribution overheads, depending on the nature of the fixtures.

28 D

The cost of the ingredients is a direct material cost.

29 B

The prime cost is the total of all direct costs which will include direct expenses as well as direct labour and materials.

30 C

The inventory valuation will be unchanged. Finished goods are valued at the total production cost and the rent is a distribution cost.

31 A

The graph shows a reduction in unit variable costs beyond certain output levels. Only Answer A is consistent with this cost behaviour pattern.

32 B

Managers are not usually classified as direct labour.

33 C

Item B describes the costs of an activity or cost centre. Item A describes cost units. Item D describes budget centres. A cost centre is defined as 'a production or service location, function, activity or item of equipment for which costs are accumulated'.

34 C

	$
Total cost of 18,500 hours	251,750
Total cost of 17,000 hours	246,500
Variable cost of 1,500 hours	5,250

Variable cost per machine hour = $5,250/1,500 machine hours = $3.50.

	$
Total cost of 17,000 hours	246,500
Less variable cost of 17,000 hours (× $3.50)	59,500
Balance = fixed costs	187,000

35   A

The cost is direct as it can be directly attributed to a job. It is an expense because it is invoiced to the company and not a payroll cost.

36   A

	Cost per unit ($) (125 units)	Cost per unit ($) (180 units)
T1	8.00	7.00
T2	14.00	14.00
T3	19.80	15.70
T4	25.80	25.80

Cost types T2 and T4 are variable and T1 and T3 are semi-variable.

37   A

	$
Total cost of 15,100 square metres	83,585
Total cost of 12,750 square metres	73,950
Variable cost of 2,350 square metres	9,635

Variable cost is $9,635/2,350 square metres = $4.10 per square metre.

Fixed costs can be found by substitution:

	$
Total cost of 12,750 square metres	73,950
Variable cost of 12,750 square metres (× $4.10)	52,275
Fixed costs	21,675

So for 16,200 square metres:

Overheads   = $21,675 + (16,200 × $4.10)

= $88,095

38   A

39   B

	$
Total cost of 10,000 units	400,000
Total cost of 5,000 units	250,000
Variable cost of 5,000 units	150,000

Therefore the variable cost per unit = $150,000/5,000 units = $30 per unit.

40   **C**

	units		$
Total cost of	20,000	=	40,000
Total cost of	4,000	=	20,000
Therefore variable cost of	16,000	=	20,000

Variable cost per unit = $20,000/16,000 units = $1.25 per unit.

41   **D**

Graph D is consistent with the cost behaviour for total materials given.

Graph A implies that there is a certain range of activity (just above 15,000 units) when total materials cost is constant.

Graph B implies that total materials cost falls beyond 15,000 units of activity.

Graph C implies that the lower cost per unit for materials applies only to units purchased in excess of 15,000.

42   **A**

For the first 10 hours of calls only the fixed line rental is charged therefore the answer cannot be B or D, which show no costs until a number of hours have passed. Graph C shows a variable cost is charged from nil to a maximum number of hours which is incorrect. The answer is A.

43   **C**

Use the two levels of production above 1,100 units per month for the high-low analysis as at these levels fixed costs are the same.

Units	Total cost ($)
1,400	68,200
1,200	66,600
200	1,600

Variable cost per unit = ($1,600 ÷ 200) = $8

Total fixed cost (above 1,100 units) = [$68,200 − (1,400 × $8)] = $57,000

Total cost for 1,000 units = [($57,000 − $6,000) + (1,000 × $8)] = $59,000

ORDERING AND ACCOUNTING FOR INVENTORY

44   C

{[Buffer Inventory + (EOQ ÷2)] × Annual holding cost per component}

= [700 units + (1500 units÷2)] × $3.00 = $4,350

45   C

Materials inventory account

	$000s		$000s
Opening inventory	15	Issued to production	165
Payables for purchases	176	Returned to suppliers	8
Returned to stores	9	Written off	4
		Closing balance (balancing item)	23
	200		200

46   D

Option A: A stores ledger account records details of receipts and issues

Option B: A stores requisition will also detail quantity required

Option C: Lead time is the time between placing an order and receiving goods

47   B

Continuous stocktaking is being described. Perpetual inventory involves recording, as they occur, receipts, issues and the resulting balances of individual items of inventory, in either quantity, or quantity and value.

48   B

Indirect materials are overhead costs so debit production overhead. An issue of materials is a credit from the material control account

49   C

A purchase order will be raised by the stores department and sent to the supplier.

50   A

Materials inventory account

	$000s		$000s
Opening inventory	23	Issued to production	144
Purchases (bal fig)	131		
Returned to stores	5		
		Closing balance (balancing item)	15
	159		159

51 B

Standard costs are used to help control the costs of purchases. Regular stocktakes and physical security help to minimise losses from stores.

52 A

In times of rising prices FIFO will give a higher valuation of the closing inventory as the older lower prices will be issued to production.

Opening inventory + units purchased	440
Units sold	(290)
Closing inventory (units)	150

FIFO	Closing inventory: 150 units @ $2.78	$417

AVCO	Weighted average cost	$
	100 units @ $2.52	252
	140 units @ $2.56	358
	200 units @ $2.78	556
	440	1,166

Average cost per unit	1,116/440	$2.65

Closing inventory: 150 units @ $2.65	$397.50
FIFO higher by (417 – 397.50)	$19.50

53 B

- If prices have fallen during the year, AVCO will give a higher value of closing inventory than FIFO, which values goods for resale at the latest prices.
- Where the value of closing inventory is higher, profits are higher.

54 B

	Items	Unit value	
		$	$
Opening inventory	6	15	90
January: purchases	10	19.80	198
	16	18	288
February: sales	(10)	18	(180)
	6	18	108
March: purchases	20	24.50	490
	26	23	598
March: sales	(5)	23	(115)
	21	23	483

		$
Sales (15 × $30)		450
Cost of sales		
Opening Inventory	90	
Purchases	688	
Closing Inventory	(483)	
		(295)
Gross profit		155

55 C

Date		Units	Unit value $	Inventory value $
1 October	Opening inventory	60		720
8 October	Purchase 40 units at $15	40		600
14 October	Purchase 50 units at $18	50		900
		150	14.80	2,220
21 October	Sold 75 units: cost	(75)	14.80	(1,110)
31 October	Closing inventory	75	14.80	1,110

56 D

The closing inventory of 12 items (15 − 5 + 10 − 8) comprise

	$
10 items at $3.50 each	35.00
2 items at $3 each	6.00
Cost on a FIFO basis is	41.00

57 A

When prices are rising, FIFO will give a higher valuation for closing inventory, because the closing inventory will consist of the most recently-purchased items. Higher closing inventory means lower cost of sales and higher profit.

ORDER QUANTITIES AND REORDER LEVELS

58 A

The formula for the EOQ has the holding cost as the denominator. If this increases, the EOQ will be lower. A lower EOQ means that more orders will have to be placed each year; therefore, the total annual ordering cost will increase.

59   C

		$
Purchase costs	(20,000 units × $40)	800,000
Order costs	(20,000/500 orders × $25/order)	1,000
Holding costs	(500/2 average units × $4/unit)	1,000
		———
Total costs		802,000
		———

60   C

Maximum usage × maximum lead time = 520 × 15 = 7,800 units

61   B

Average inventory   = ROQ/2 + minimum inventory

= 100/2 + 20 = 70 chairs

62   D

The economic batch quantity determines the batch size for products manufactured internally. The EBQ is the batch size which minimises the total of inventory holding costs and batch set-up costs.

63   B

$$\text{Economic batch quantity} = \sqrt{\frac{2C_oD}{C_h\left(1-\dfrac{D}{R}\right)}}$$

$$= \sqrt{\frac{2(1,500)(40,000)}{25\left(1-\dfrac{40,000}{100,000}\right)}}$$

$$= \sqrt{\frac{120\,\text{million}}{15}}$$

$$= \sqrt{8,000,000}$$

= 2,828 units.

64   A

The EOQ model distinguishes between holding costs (i and ii) and ordering costs (iii)

65   C

Annual holding cost = {[Buffer inventory + (EOQ ÷2)] x Annual holding cost per component}

= {[500 + (2000 ÷2)] x2}   = 3,000

66   A

Let O = ordering cost

$185 = \sqrt{\{[\,2 \times O \times (4 \times 2{,}000)\,] \div [0.05 \times 42]\}}$

$185 = \sqrt{(16{,}000 \times O \div 2.1)}$

$O = 185^2 \times 2.1 \div 16{,}000 = \$4.49$

Note that the period for demand must be the same as that given for holding cost. As holding cost is given as an annual figure quarterly demand must be converted to annual demand by multiplying by 4.

67   C

Using the formula given: EOQ $= \sqrt{[(2 \times 120 \times 48{,}000) \div (0.10 \times 80)]} = 1{,}200$ units

68   A

		$
Purchasing cost (48,000 × $80)		3,840,000
Ordering cost (48,000 ÷ 1,200) × $120		4,800
Holding costs [(1,200 ÷ 2) × $80 × 0.10]		4,800
Total cost		3,849,600

69   C

	$
Purchasing cost (48,000 × $80 × 0.99)	3,801,600
Ordering cost (48,000 ÷ 2,000) × $120	2,880
Holding costs [(2,000 ÷ 2) × $80 × 0.99 × 0.10]	7,920
Total cost	3,812,400

Annual total saving = $(3,849,600 – 3,812,400) $37,200

70   C

Order quantity = 750 units

			$
Order cost	600 × 12 × 8.75/750 =		84
Holding cost	0.1 × 2.24 × 750/2 =		84
Purchase cost	600 × 12 × 2.24 =		16,128
Total cost			16,296

Order quantity = 2,000 units

		$
Order cost	$600 \times 12 \times 8.75/2,000 =$	31.50
Holding cost	$0.1 \times 2.24 \times 0.95 \times 2,000/2 =$	212.80
Purchase cost	$600 \times 12 \times 2.24 \times 0.95 =$	15,321.60
		————
		15,565.90

Change in cost = $16,296 − $15,566 = saving of $730.

71   C

Annual production rate = $500 \times 50 = 25,000$

Using the economic batch quantity formula given,

$2,000 = \sqrt{\{(2 \times \text{setup cost} \times 5,000)/(1.5 \times (1-5,000/25,000))\}}$

Setup cost = $2000 \times 2000 \times 1.5 \times 0.8/(2 \times 5,000) = \$480$

ACCOUNTING FOR LABOUR

72   A

Statement (i) is correct, because extra spending would be incurred to pay the additional temporary staff. Statement (ii) is incorrect, because total spending on labour is unaffected when spare capacity is utilised and idle time reduced. Statement (iii) is also incorrect, because total labour costs will not be increased by switching labour from working on one product to working on another product. However, there is an opportunity cost in switching labour. This is the total contribution forgone by no longer producing and selling the original product. This opportunity cost would be a relevant cost in evaluating a decision to switch the labour from one product to the other. Even so, as worded, statement (iii) is incorrect.

73   B

Unless the overtime can be traced to a specific product or job, it will be treated as an indirect production cost and absorbed into units using the normal absorption basis.

74   B

The employee took 44 hours to perform 94 operations. The standard time allowed per operation is 37.5 minutes, giving a standard time of $(94 \times [37.5/60]) = 58.75$ hours to perform 94 operations. The time saved is therefore $(58.75 − 44) = 14.75$ hours. The bonus payable will be:

(time taken/time allowed) $\times$ time saved $\times$ hourly rate

$= (44/58.75) \times 14.75 \times \$6.50 = \$71.80$ (rounded).

The gross wage for Week 24 will therefore be $(44 \text{ hours} \times \$6.50) + \$71.80 = \$357.80$.

75   A

Direct labour costs are credited to wages and salaries and debited to work-in-progress.

76   D

$240,000 ÷0.80 = $300,000

77   C

If direct labour is working at below the agreed productivity level, this will lead to lower output than planned. This could have been caused by factors which resulted in idle time, such as (ii) and (iii) but would not lead to idle time.

78   B

40 × $15 = $600. Note that the basic element of overtime is classified as a direct cost. The normal treatment of overtime premium is for it to be treated as an indirect cost.

79   B

Average employment during the year was (5,250 + 5,680) / 2 = 5,465

The labour turnover rate = 360/5,465 × 100% = 6.6%

80   D

Expected hours to make actual output/actual hours = 192/180 × 100% = 106.7%

81   D

Actual hours/budget hours = 180/185 × 100% = 97.3%

82   C

Expected hours to make actual output/budget hours = 192/185 × 100% = 103.8%

ACCOUNTING FOR OVERHEADS

83   B

Reapportion service cost centre K first as it does work for service cost centre J but not vice versa.

	G	H	J	K
Overhead cost ($)	40,000	50,000	30,000	18,000
Reapportion K	9,000	7,200	1,800	(18,000)
			31,800	
Reapportion J	9,540		(31,800)	
	$58,540			

84 C

An absorption rate is used to determine the full cost of a product or service. Answer A describes overhead allocation and apportionment. Absorption does not control overheads, so answer D is not correct.

85 D

X = 46,000 + 0.1Y

Y = 30,000 + 0.2X

X = 46,000 + 0.1(30,000 + 0.2X) = 46,000 + 3,000 + 0.02X

0.98X = 49,000 and X = 50,000

Y = 30,000 + 0.2(50,000) = 40,000

P = 95,000 + 0.4(50,000) + 0.3(40,000) = 127,000

Alternatively use the repeated distribution method as follows;

	P	Q	X	Y
Overhead cost ($)	95,000	82,000	46,000	30,000
Reapportion X	18,400	18,400	(46,000)	9,200
Reapportion Y	11,760	23,520	3,920	(39,200)
Reapportion X	1,568	1,568	(3,920)	784
Reapportion Y	235	470	78	(784)
Reapportion X	31	31	(78)	16
Reapportion Y	5	9	2	(16)
Rounding	1	1		
	$127,000			

86 B

	$
Actual expenditure	56,389
Absorbed cost (12,400 × 1.02 × $4.25)	53,754
Total under-absorption	2,635

87 A

Under- or over-absorption is determined by comparing the actual overhead expenditure with the overhead absorbed.

88 D

Fixed production overheads are over-absorbed when actual expenditure is less than budget and/or actual production volume is higher than budget.

89   D

Over-absorbed overheads increase profit, and so are recorded as a credit entry in either an over-absorbed overhead account or directly as a credit in the income statement. The matching debit entry could be either in the WIP account or the production overhead control account, depending on the costing system used.

90   C

Indirect labour is a costing concept. The double entry is:

Wages control		Overhead control	
	Indirect labour × (overheads)	Indirect labour × (wages)	

91   A

Machining hours	=	$(4,000 \times 0.5 \text{ hour}) + (4,000 \times 1.0 \text{ hour})$
	=	6,000 hours
Assembly hours	=	$(4,000 \times 0.2 \text{ hour}) + (4,000 \times 0.25 \text{ hour})$
	=	1,800 hours
Machining absorption rate	=	$\dfrac{\$120,000}{6,000 \text{ hours}}$
	=	$20 per hour
Assembly absorption rate	=	$\dfrac{\$72,000}{1,800 \text{ hours}}$
	=	$40 per hour
Fixed overhead per unit of Pye	=	$(0.5 \text{ hour} \times \$20) + (0.2 \text{ hour} \times \$40)$
	=	$18

92   D

Cost apportionment is concerned with sharing costs according to benefit received.

93   B

	$
Actual overheads	694,075
Under recovery	(35,000)
Overhead absorbed	659,075

OAR	=	$\dfrac{\$659,075}{32,150}$
	=	$20.50

94 B

	$
Actual overheads	245,600
Over-absorption of overheads	6,400
Overheads absorbed	252,000

Absorption rate = $252,000/45,000 hours = $5.60 per direct labour hour.

95 D

	$
Actual overhead	138,000
Over-absorbed overhead	23,000
Therefore amount of overhead absorbed	161,000

Hours worked = 11,500.

Therefore absorption rate per hour = $161,000/11,500 hours = $14 per hour.

96 C

Let the overhead apportioned from service department C be $C.

Let the overhead apportioned from service department D be $D.

$$C = 3,200 + 0.20D \;.....(1)$$
$$D = 4,600 + 0.10 C \;....(2)$$

Substitute (1) in (2)

$$D = 4,600 + 0.10(3,200 + 0.20D)$$

$$D = 4,600 + 320 + 0.02D$$

$$0.98D = 4,920$$

$$D = 5,020.$$

Substitute in (1)

$$C = 3,200 + 0.20 (5,020)$$

$$C = 4,204.$$

Total overhead for department X = 5,000 + 0.50C + 0.20D

$$= 5,000 + 0.50(4,204) + 0.20 (5,020)$$

$$= 5,000 + 2,102 + 1,004$$

$$= 8,106.$$

Allowing for a rounding difference, this is answer C.

Note: You could have reached the same answer by using the repeated distribution method.

97 B

Fixed overhead absorption rate = $36,000/18,000 = $2 per direct labour hour.

Variable overhead absorption rate = $9,000/18,000 = $0.50 per direct labour hour.

	$	$
Overheads absorbed:		
Fixed (20,000 × $2)		40,000
Variable (20,000 × $0.50)		10,000
Total overhead absorbed		50,000
Overheads incurred:		
Fixed	39,000	
Variable	12,000	
Total overhead incurred		51,000
Under-absorbed overhead		1,000

98 B

$$(\$3,000 \times \frac{700}{8,000}) + (\$11,000 \times \frac{80}{400}) + (\$7,000 \times \frac{20}{70}) = \$(262.50 + 2,200 + 2,000) = \$4,462.50$$

99 C

$$60 \times \frac{12}{120} + 100 \times \frac{8}{100} = \$14$$

MARGINAL AND ABSORPTION COSTING

100 C

Total variable cost	= $(4 + 5 + 3 + 3) = $15
Contribution per unit	= $20 − $15 = $5
Total contribution earned	= $5 × 800 = $4,000

101 D

If a sales value of $100 per unit is assumed then the original and revised situations will be:

	Original	Revised
	$	$
Selling price	100	110
Variable cost/unit	60	60
Contribution/unit	40	50

Fixed costs do not affect contribution and if sales volume is unchanged then the overall change in contribution can be measured using the contribution per unit:

$$\frac{(50-40)}{40} = 25\%$$

102 D

Absorption costing profit = $2,000 > Marginal Costing profit = $(3,000)

Therefore Production > Sales by $5,000

$5,000 = OAR x number of units change in stock

$5,000 = $2 x number of units change in stock

Therefore number of units change in stock = $\dfrac{\$5,000}{\$2}$ = 2,500

If Sales = 10,000 units, therefore Production = Sales + 10,000 units = 12,500 units.

103 B

Contribution per unit = $(10 – 6) = $4.

	$
Total contribution (250,000 × $4)	1,000,000
Fixed overheads (200,000 × $2)	400,000
Profit	600,000

104 B

Fixed production overhead per unit = $48,000/12,000 units = $4.

Sales volume is less than production volume by 280 units.

In absorption costing, this means that some fixed overheads will be carried forward in the closing inventory value. Fixed overheads in this addition to inventory = 280 units × $4 = $1,120.

In marginal costing, all fixed overheads incurred in a period are charged as an expense against profit. Marginal costing profit would therefore be lower than the absorption costing profit by $1,120.

105 B

As inventory decreases over the period, the cost of sales will be higher with absorption costing, since they will include fixed overhead in the opening inventory now sold. The extra cost of sales (and thus reduction in profit) = (8,500 – 6,750) × $3 = $5,250.

This means that since profit will be lower with absorption costing by $5,250, the absorption costing profit will be $(62,100 – 5,250) = $56,850.

106 C

There was an increase in inventory in the period; therefore the absorption costing profit is higher than the marginal costing profit (because a larger amount of fixed overhead is carried forward in the closing inventory value).

	$
Marginal costing profit	72,300
Less: fixed costs in opening inventory (300 units × $5)	(1,500)
Add: fixed costs in closing inventory (750 units × $5)	3,750
Absorption costing profit	74,550

107 B

Production volume exceeded sales volume, so the profit with absorption costing is higher than the profit with marginal costing.

Fixed overheads in inventory = $30,000/750 = $40 per unit, therefore total fixed overhead in closing inventory (absorption costing) = 250 units × $40 = $10,000. Profit with marginal costing is therefore lower by $10,000.

108 D

		$000
Variable production cost of boats	45/750×700	42
Fixed production costs (absorbed)	30/750×700	28
Production costs of 700 boats		70
Closing inventory of 100 boats		(10)
Production cost of 600 sold		60
Under-absorbed overhead	30-28	2
Variable selling costs	5/500×600	6
Fixed selling costs		25
		93
Profit		15
Sales revenue	90/500×600	108

109 B

The marginal cost of a product is the additional cost of producing an extra unit and is therefore the sum of the variable costs. If the inventory increases over a year, absorption costing profit will be higher than marginal costing profit because an element of fixed cost will be carried forward in closing inventory to be charged against profit in a future period.

110 B

In an absorption costing system, the fixed cost per unit would be $3,000/15,000 units = $0.20 per unit.

Budgeted profit with marginal costing = Contribution − Fixed costs

= $26,000 − $3,000 = $23,000.

By switching to absorption costing, in a period when inventory levels increase by 2,000 units, absorption costing profit would be higher by 2,000 units × fixed cost per unit, i.e. by 2,000 × $0.20 = $400.

Absorption costing profit = $23,000 + $400 = $23,400.

111 A

Total contribution will increase as sales volume increases, but the contribution per unit will be constant as long as the sales price and variable cost per unit are unchanged. Overhead is not absorbed to product unit so there is no under/over absorption of overhead. Marginal costing does provide useful information for decision making because it highlights contribution, which is a relevant cash flow for decision-making purposes.

112 C

Increase in inventory of 34,000 − 31,000 = 3,000 units.

Difference in profits of $955,500 − $850 500 = $105,000

OAR = $105,000/3,000 = $35 per unit

Level of activity = $1,837,500/£35 = 52,500 units

113 A

Profit figures only differ if inventory changes in the period.

114 C

Point C is where total revenue exceeds total costs by the largest amount, i.e. where profit is maximised.

115 B

Suppose we start with the following situation.

	$ per unit
Selling price	100
Variable cost	(60)
Contribution	40

Sales 1,000 units; total contribution $40,000

A, B and C would have the following effects.

	A $ per unit	B $ per unit
Selling price	100	110
Variable cost	(54)	(60)
Contribution	46	50
Total contribution	$46,000	$50,000

C : Total contribution = $40,000 × 1.1

= $44,000

Fixed costs are irrelevant since we are concerned with *contribution*.

116 B

Inventory is valued at full production cost i.e. both fixed and variable production costs.

$(33.00 + 45.10) = $78.10

JOB, BATCH AND PROCESS COSTING

117 C

	Job 812 $
Direct materials	60
Direct labour	40
Direct expenses	20
Prime cost	120
Production overheads ($40 ÷ 8) × $16	80
Non-production overheads (0.6 × $120)	72
Total cost – Job 812	272

118 D

Statement A is correct. Job costs are identified with a particular job, whereas process costs (of units produced and work in process) are averages, based on equivalent units of production.

Statement B is also correct. The direct cost of a job to date, excluding any direct expenses, can be ascertained from materials requisition notes and job tickets or time sheets.

Statement C is correct, because without data about units completed and units still in process, losses and equivalent units of production cannot be calculated.

Statement D is incorrect, because the cost of normal loss will usually be incorporated into job costs as well as into process costs. In process costing this is commonly done by giving normal loss no cost, leaving costs to be shared between output, closing inventory and abnormal loss/gain. In job costing it can be done by adjusting direct materials costs to allow for normal wastage, and direct labour costs for normal reworking of items or normal spoilage.

119 D

	Job 1	Job 2	Total
	$	$	$
Opening WIP	8,500	0	8,500
Material in period	17,150	29,025	46,175
Labour for period	12,500	23,000	35,500
Overheads (see working)	43,750	80,500	124,250
	81,900	132,525	214,425

Working

Total labour cost for period = $(12,500 + 23,000 + 4,500) = $40,000

Overhead absorption rate = $140,000/$40,000 = 3.5 times the direct labour cost.

120 C

	Job 3
	$
Opening WIP	46,000
Labour cost for period	4,500
Overheads (3.5 × $4,500)	15,750
Total production costs	66,250
Profit (50%)	33,125
Selling price of 2,400 boards	99,375

Selling price of one board = $99,375/2,400 = $41.41

121 D

This can be calculated as a balancing figure in the process account.

Process account

	kg		$		kg		$
Input (balance)	3,000		21,150	Output	2,800	(× 7.50)	21,000
Abnormal gain	100	(× 7.50)	750	Normal loss	300	(× 3)	900
			21,900				21,900

Alternatively:

	$
Cost of output (2,800 × 7.50)	21,000
Scrap value of normal loss (300 × 3)	900
	21,900
Less: Value of abnormal gain (100 × 7.50)	(750)
Cost of input	21,150

122   B

	Units
Input	13,200
Less: Normal loss (13,200 × 10/110)	1,200
Expected output	12,000

	$
Process costs	184,800
Less: scrap value of normal loss (1,200 × $4)	4,800
Cost of good output	180,000

Cost for each expected unit of output = $180,000/12,000 = $15.

Finished units of output, and also abnormal loss and abnormal gain units will be valued at this amount.

123   B

Cost per unit = net process costs/expected output

= (9,000 + 13,340 + 300)/ 2,000 -100

= $22,040/1,900 = $11.60.

124   A

	$
Opening WIP	1,710
Completion of opening WIP (300 × 0.40 × $10)	1,200
Units started and completed in the month	
(2,000 – 300) × $10	17,000
Total value (2,000 units)	19,910

125   C

	Materials equivalent units
Opening inventory completed (400 × 0%)	0
Units started and finished in the period (800 – 400)	400
Closing inventory (600 × 75%)	450
Total equivalent units produced in the period	850

126 D

Sales value of production :

Product W : (12,000 x 10) = $120,000
Product X : (10,000 x 12) = $120,000

Therefore joint production costs are apportioned W:X in the ratio 1:1
Amount apportioned to product X is (776,160 ÷2) = $388,080
20% of X's production is in closing inventory @ (0.2 x 388,080) = $77,616

Answer B has split the joint production costs on the basis of sales prices and Answer C has used the sales value of sales to apportion joint production costs.

127 D

	Units
J: (6,000 – 100 + 300) =	6,200
K: (4,000 – 400 + 200) =	3,800
	10,000

Joint costs apportioned to J: (6,200 ÷ 10,000) × $110,000 = $68,200

128 C

Total sales revenue = ($18 × 10,000) + ($25 × 20,000) + ($20 × 20,000) = $1,080,000	
Joint costs to be allocated	= $277,000 – ($2 × 3,500)
	= $270,000

Allocation rate = ($270,000/1,080,000) = 0.25 of sales revenue.

Joint costs allocated to product 3	= 0.25 × ($20 × 20,000)
	= $100,000
	= ($100,000/20,000 units) $5 per unit

129 C

		$
Prime cost		6,840.00
Fixed overhead	$300,000/60,000 × 156	780.00
		7,620.00
Profit	20% × 7,620.00	1,524.00
Job price		9,144.00

130 D

Abnormal loss units are valued as one equivalent unit of cost, the same as units of good production. This cost is credited to the process account and debited to the abnormal loss account. The scrap value of abnormal loss is then credited to the abnormal loss account (with the matching debit to bank).

131 A

		kg
Input		12,750
Output	Normal loss	510
	Finished goods	12,700
		13,210
Abnormal gain		460

132 A

	kg
Material input	2,500
Normal loss (10%)	(250)
Abnormal loss	(75)
Good production achieved	2,175

133 C

Direct labour hours = $400 ÷ $8 = 50 hours

	$
Prime cost (300 + 400)	700
Production overheads (50 × $26)	1,300
Total production cost	2,000
Non-production overheads (1.20 × 700)	840
Total cost	2,840

134 B

Finished output = (20,000 + 110,000 – 40,000) = 90,000 units.

Closing WIP = 40,000 units 50% complete = 20,000 equivalent units.

Cost per equivalent unit (in $000) = $132,000/(90,000 + 20,000)

= $1,200 per equivalent unit/finished car.

135 B

The total value of WIP will increase. The number of equivalent units will increase which will cause the cost per unit to decrease.

136   C

Normal loss is 10% of input = 20 kg.

Actual loss = 50 kg

Abnormal loss = 50 – 20 = 30 kg

Equivalent units of output:

	Total	Materials	Conversion
Finished output	150	150	150
Abnormal loss	30	30	15
Total EUs	180	180	165

Cost per equivalent unit:

Material cost = 200 × $ 4 = $800
Labour and overheads cost = 100× $ 15 + $1,000 = $2,500

Materials   = $800/180 = $4.44
Conversion   = $2,500/165 = $15.15

Total cost of completed unit = $(4.44 + 15.15) = $19.59

137   A

Process account

	Units		Units
Opening WIP	2,000	Finished	11,000
Started	12,000	Closing WIP	3,000
	____		____
	14,000		14,000

Units started and finished = 11,000 – 2,000	=	9,000
Closing WIP = 3,000 x 20%	=	600
Opening WIP = 2,000 x 30%	=	600
		10,200

138   C

Cost per unit = (1,200 + 3,500 – 30) / 200 – 30 = 27.47 per kg

27.47 × 190 = $5,219

139   A

Process costing is used for companies producing large quantities of similar products (homogeneous output) and these are valued at average cost.

140 A

	$
Direct materials 120 kg @ $4 per kg	480
Direct labour: 3 hours @ $10 per hour	30
20 hours @ $5 per hour	100
Hire of machine: 2 days @ $100 per day	200
Overhead 23 hours @ $8 per hour	184
	994
Price charged	942
Loss	(52)

SERVICE AND OPERATION COSTING

141 C

A service industry is an industry not involved in agriculture, mining, construction or manufacturing. Transport industries are service industries.

142 C

Services are usually (but not always) associated with labour and labour costs, low material costs and relatively high indirect costs. Service costing also makes use of composite cost units, such as the cost per guest/day, cost per patient/day, cost per passenger/mile and so on.

143 D

A charitable foundation will be a not-for-profit organisation.

144 B

Average cost per occupied bed per day

$$= \frac{\text{Total cost}}{\text{Number of beds occupied}}$$

$$= \frac{\$100,000 + \$5,000 + \$22,500}{6,450 \times 2} = \$9.88$$

or $127,500/(200 \times 2 + 30) \times 30 = \$9.88$

145 B

	$	$
Cost per:		
Millions of units sold	208	104
Thousand consumers	750	625
$m of sales	33,333	20,000

The cost per unit sold, per consumer and per $m of sales are all higher for Company A than for Company B indicating that Company A is less efficient than Company B.

146 B

$$\text{Room occupancy \%} = \frac{\text{Total number of rooms occupied daily}}{\text{Rooms available to be let}} \times 100\%$$

$$= \frac{200 + 30}{240 + 40} \times 100\% = 82.1\%$$

147 C

A service is intangible and inventory cannot be held. Services generally have a high level of fixed costs and there are often difficulties in identifying a suitable cost unit.

ALTERNATIVE COSTING PRINCIPLES

148 A

ABC is fairly complicated, is a form of absorption (not marginal) costing and is particularly useful when fixed overheads are high and not primarily volume driven.

149 D

A customer service team deals with customer queries and complaints from outside the organisation, typically after goods have been delivered to the customer. The costs of this team arise from quality failures and are preventable. They are external failure costs. Maintenance is intended to prevent machine breakdowns and so to prevent quality failures, and they are therefore prevention costs. Test equipment is used for inspection.

150 C

External failure costs are those incurred due to poor quality of goods delivered to customers; therefore this includes compensation costs.

Appraisal costs are those incurred in the measuring of quality of output; therefore this includes test equipment running costs.

151 B

	$
Sales revenue: 600 units × $450	450
Return required: 20% × $450	90

Target cost per unit:	360

152 D

A product's life cycle costs are very inclusive; none of these would be excluded.

153 A

Value analysis involves identify why and how customers value a product to enable cost savings to be made without compromising the value to the customer.

154 B

FORECASTING TECHNIQUES

155 A

As advertising will hopefully generate sales, advertising is the independent variable and sales revenue the dependent; i.e. advertising is x and sales revenue is y.

		$
High	Sales revenue from $6,500 of advertising	225,000
Low	Sales revenue from $2,500 of advertising	125,000
	Marginal sales revenue from $4,000 of advertising	100,000

Marginal sales revenue for each $1 of advertising = $100,000/$4,000 = $25.

	$
Sales revenue from $6,500 of advertising	225,000
Marginal sales revenue from $6,500 of advertising (× $25)	162,500
Fixed sales revenue (even with no advertising)	62,500

This gives a function of sales revenue = $62,500 + $25x, where x is the spending on advertising.

156 C

In the formula C = 1,000 + 250P, 1,000 represents the weekly fixed costs and 250 the variable cost per unit.

157 B

C= F + Vx

14,520 = 7,788 + V(3,300)

6,732= 3,300V

V= 2.04

158 A

Coefficient of determination = r^2 = 0.6 × 0.6 = 0.36 = 36%

159 B

$$a = \frac{\sum y}{n} - \frac{b\sum x}{n}$$

$$a = \frac{183.0}{5} - \frac{4.2(21)}{5} = [36.6 - 17.64] = 18.96.$$

If there are 5 salesmen in the month, expected costs will be, in $000:

18.96 + (4.2 × 5) = **39.96**.

160 A

This question is a simple test of your understanding of the meaning of the elements in a regression analysis formula. Statements (i) and (ii) are correct, but statement (iii) is wrong. The total value of x multiplied by the total value of y would be written as $\Sigma x\ \Sigma y$, not as Σxy.

161 B

You should use the formulae provided in the examination (formulae sheet)

$$b = \frac{11 \times 13{,}467 - (440 \times 330)}{(11 \times 17{,}986) - (440)^2} = \frac{2{,}937}{4{,}246} = 0.6917$$

162 B

$\Sigma x = \Sigma$ Advertising expenditure = 100,000

$\Sigma y = \Sigma$ Sales revenue = 600,000

n = number of pairs of data = 5

163 A

164 B

$\Sigma y = 17{,}500 + 19{,}500 + 20{,}500 + 18{,}500 + 17{,}000 = 93{,}000$

$\Sigma x = 300 + 360 + 400 + 320 + 280 = 1{,}660$

$a = (93{,}000 \div 5) - 29.53(1{,}660 \div 5) = 8{,}796.04$

165 B

+1 represents perfect positive correlation.

−1 represents perfect negative correlation.

The nearer to 0 the correlation coefficient the less correlation between the variables.

166 A

$$b = \frac{n \Sigma xy - \Sigma x \Sigma y}{n \Sigma x^2 - (\Sigma x)^2}$$

$$= [(5 \times 23{,}091) - (129 \times 890)] \div [(5 \times 3{,}433) - (129^2)] = 1.231$$

$$a = \frac{\Sigma y}{n} - b\frac{\Sigma x}{n}$$

$$= (890 \div 5) - [(1.231 \times 129) \div 5] = 146 \text{ (nearest whole number)}$$

167 B

The correlation coefficient must be between +1 and −1.

168 C

169 A

Quarter	'Real' sales
1	$\dfrac{109}{100} \times 100 = 109.0$
2	$\dfrac{120}{110} \times 100 = 109.1$
3	$\dfrac{132}{121} \times 100 = 109.1$
4	$\dfrac{145}{133} \times 100 = 109.0$

The 'real' series is approximately constant and keeping up with inflation.

170 C

Current cost = $5 \times 430 \div 150$

171 B

	P_0	P_1	Q_1	P_1Q_1	P_0Q_1
Flour	0.25	0.30	10,000	3,000	2,500
Eggs	1.00	1.25	5,000	6,250	5,000
Milk	0.30	0.35	10,000	3,500	3,000
Potatoes	0.05	0.06	10,000	600	500
				13,350	11,000

$$= \frac{13,350}{11,000} \times 100 = 121.36$$

172 C

	P_0	P_1	Q_0	P_1Q_0	P_0Q_0
Flour	0.25	0.30	8,000	2,400	2,000
Eggs	1.00	1.25	4,000	5,000	4,000
Milk	0.30	0.35	10,000	3,500	3,000
Potatoes	0.05	0.06	6,000	360	300
				11,260	9,300

$$= \frac{11,260}{9,300} \times 100 = 121.08$$

173 C

see table below

174 D

see table below

	Sales volume (units)	Trend	Variation
January	172,100		
February	149,600		
March	165,800	166,040	−240
April	182,600	171,040	11,560
May	160,100	176,040	−15,940
June	197,100	181,040	16,060
July	174,600	186,040	−11,440
August	190,800	191,040	−240
September	207,600	196,040	11,560
October		201,040	−15,940
November		206,040	16,060
December	199,600	211,040	−11,440

175 D

176 A

($2,000 × 120 ÷ 160) = $1,500

177 B

(5,000 + 23 × 4,000 − 1,500) = 95,500

178 A

$y = a + bx$

$y = 3,000 + (150 × 3)$

$y = 3,450$

Actual − trend = variation

3,500 − 3,450 = +50

179 C

$y = a + bx$

$y = 3,000 + (150 × 15)$

$y = 5,250$

Trend + variation = actual

5,250 + 50 = 5,300

180 C

Development, Introduction, and Decline

181 A

	P_0	P_1	Q_0	P_1Q_0	P_0Q_0
F	11	12	21	252	231
G	22	26	56	1,456	1,232
H	18	18	62	1,116	1,116
I	20	22	29	638	580
J	22	23	31	713	682
				4,175	3,841

$$= \frac{4,175}{3,841} \times 100 = 108.7$$

182 C

	P_0	P_1	Q_1	P_1Q_1	P_0Q_1
F	11	12	25	300	275
G	22	26	52	1,352	1,144
H	18	18	79	1,422	1,422
I	20	22	35	770	700
J	22	23	36	828	792
				4,672	4,333

$$= \frac{4,672}{4,333} \times 100 = 107.8$$

BUDGETING

183 B

The main purposes of budgeting are to plan and control. Budgets also usually give authority to spend up to the budget limit. Budgets are not primarily used for decision making.

184 B

False is the correct answer because the budget committee is made up from senior managers of each function in the organisation.

185 B

Units required	100,000
Less: opening inventory	(14,000)
Add: closing inventory required (14,000 × 0.6)	8,400
	———
	94,400
	———

186 B

False is the correct answer because the production budget is the sales budget **plus** closing inventory of finished goods **minus** opening inventory of finished goods.

187 B

4,500/0.9 = 5,000 litres.

Note that opening and closing inventories are relevant to the material purchases budget, not the material usage budget.

188 A

True is the correct answer because the material usage budget is the material requirement for the units produced.

189 C

		$
Product A	1,750 units × 3 hours/unit × $7 /hour	36,750
Product B	5,000 units × 4 hours/unit × $7 /hour	140,000
		———
		176,750
		———

190 D

A principal budget factor is defined as the factor acting as the constraint on the overall level of activity in a period. It is often sales demand, but could be a key production resource or cash.

191 D

If 1X and 2Y are sold, this earns $250. Call this a batch.

The company wants to earn $100,000.

$100,000 / 250 = 400 batches.

This is 400 X and 800 Y

192 D

A budget manual will include all of the options.

193 B

	Units
Budgeted sales	2,300
Current inventory	(400)
Closing inventory required	550
	———
Production	2,450

194 A

Machine hours required:

X	1,000 hours
Y	2,400 hours
Z	600 hours
Total	4,000

Overhead budget:

Variable: $4,000 \times \$2.30 = \$9,200$

Fixed: $4,000 \times \$0.75 = \$3,000$

Total = $\$(9,200 + 3,000) = \$12,200$

195 C

	Clockwork clown	Wind-up train	Total
Budgeted sales	450	550	
+ Closing inventory	30	40	
– Opening inventory	(20)	(50)	
Production budget	460	540	
Material usage	× 2 kg	× 1 kg	
Material usage budget	920 kg	540 kg	1,460 kg

196 A

Total material usage	1,460 kg
+ Closing inventory	60
– Opening inventory	(50)
Total material purchases	1,470 kg
Material purchases budget = 1,470 × $5	$7,350

197 A

	Clockwork clown	Wind-up train
Budgeted sales	450	550
+ Closing inventory	30	40
– Opening inventory	(20)	(50)
Production budget	460	540
Labour	× 18/60	× 30/60
	138 hours	270 hours
Total	408 hours × $8 = $3,264	

198 D

Paid hours including idle time = 2,400 × 100/80 = 3,000

Budgeted labour cost = 3,000 hours × $10 = $30,000

199 C

Statement (i) is incorrect. Managers at an operational level are more likely to know what is realistically achievable than a senior manager imposing budget targets from above. Statement (ii) is arguably correct: participation in budgeting could improve motivation. Statement (iii) is correct: imposed budgets should be much quicker to prepare, because less discussion time and negotiation time is required than with participative budget-setting.

CAPITAL BUDGETING

200 C

	$	DF	$
Outflow	(80,000)	1.000	(80,000)
Cash inflow $25,000 each year for 8 years	25,000	6.463	161,575
Present value of project			$81,575

201 C

202 B

Year	Cash inflow/(outflow)	Discount factor @ 8%	Present value $
0	(60,000)	1.000	(60,000)
1	23,350	0.926	21,622
2	29,100	0.857	24,939
3	27,800	0.794	22,073
Net present value			8,634

203 C

Try 20%

Year	Cash $	20%	PV $
0	(75,000)		(75,000)
1 – 5	25,000	2.991	74,775
			(225)

IRR $= 15 + \dfrac{8,800}{(8,800+225)} \times 5$

IRR $= 15 + \dfrac{8,800}{9,025} \times 5$

IRR   = 19.88% therefore 20% to the nearest 1%

204 C

Statement A is not correct as there is no company policy to confirm the payback is appropriate. Statement B is not correct as the IRR and ROCE are not comparable. Statement D is not correct as the IRR is always a positive whether the project is acceptable or not.

Statement C is correct as the IRR must be greater than the cost of capital (the discount rate) used to appraise the project as the project has a return therefore a positive NPV at the company's cost of capital so the project should not go ahead.

205 A

Year	Cash	11%	PV
	$		$
0	(300,000)		(300,000)
1 – 10	40,000	5.889	235,560
			—————
			(64,440)

206 C

	Current			Expansion	
	$000	$000		$000	$000
Food sales	200		× 40%	80	
Drink sales	170		× 40%	68	
	———	370		———	148
Food costs	145		× 40%	58	
Drink costs	77		× 40%	31	
Staff costs	40		40/4 × 1	10	
Other costs	20		× 60% × 40%	5	
	———	282		———	104
		———			———
Cash flow		88			44

207 D

Year	Cash ($000)	17% discount factor	Present value ($000)
0	(400)	1.000	(400.00)
1	210	0.855	179.55
2	240	0.731	175.44
3	320	0.624	199.68
			———
			154.67

208 B

$$10 + \frac{\$17,706}{(\$17,706 + \$4,317)} \times (15 - 10) = 14\%$$

209 C

Depreciation is not a cash flow so needs to be added back to profit to calculate cash flows.

Depreciation on straight line basis = ($400,000 − $50,000)/5 = $70,000 per year

Year	Profit ($)	Cash flow ($)	Cumulative cash flow ($)
0		(400,000)	(400,000)
1	175,000	245,000	(155,000)
2	225,000	295,000	140,000

Payback period = 1 + 155 / 295 years = 1.5 years to nearest 0.1 years

210 D

211 D

BUDGETARY CONTROL

212 B

Option C is a fixed budget and option D is a rolling budget. Option A is incorrect as a flexible budget includes all costs.

213 C

A flexible budget helps to control resource efficiency by providing a realistic budget cost allowance for the actual level of activity achieved. Control action can therefore be more effective because the effects of any volume change have been removed from the comparison.

214 A

A fixed budget is a budget prepared for a planned single level of activity. It does not ignore inflation (option C is incorrect) and it includes direct costs as well as overhead costs (option D is incorrect). A fixed budget can be prepared for a single product as well as a mix of products (option B is incorrect).

215 B

Statement (i) is correct. A fixed budget is prepared for a single level of activity.

Statement (ii) is incorrect. A flexible budget is prepared during the budget period but it recognises only the effects of changes in the volume of activity.

Statement (iii) is correct. A major purpose of the budgetary planning exercise is to communicate an organisation's objectives to its managers.

216 B

False is the correct answer because the volume variance is the difference between the fixed and flexible budget.

217 B

Flexed budget:

	Budget	Flexed Budget	Actual
Sales (units)	120,000	100,000	100,000
	$000	$000	$000
Sales revenue	1,200	1,000	995
Variable printing costs	360	300	280
Variable production overheads	60	50	56
Fixed production cost	300	300	290
Fixed administration cost	360	360	364
Profit/(Loss)	120	(10)	5

218 A

The expenditure variance is measured by the difference between the flexed budget and the actual cost.

The expenditure variance is $15,000 favourable.

The volume variance is measured by the difference between the original budget and the flexed budget.

The volume variance is $130,000 adverse.

219 B

Machine rental is more likely to be arranged at a higher level

220 D

The production-line manager does not control prices or rates

STANDARD COSTING

221 D

All the techniques listed in the question could be used to monitor and control costs.

222 C

The standard labour rate should be the expected rate/hour, but allowing for standard levels of idle time. For example, if the work force is paid $9 per hour but idle time of 10% is expected, the standard labour rate will be $10 per hour, not $9.

223 D

Standard contribution on actual sales	$10,000
Add : favourable sales price variance	$500
Less : Adverse total variable costs variance	$(2,000)
Actual Contribution	**$8,500**

The standard contribution on actual sales has been obtained by adjusting the budgeted contribution by the sales volume contribution variance. Therefore, this variance should have been ignored in answering the question.

224 A

Sales contribution on actual sales	$50,000
Less adverse total variable costs variance	$3,500
Actual contribution	$46,500

No adjustment is required for the favourable sales volume contribution variance : it would have already been added to the budgeted contribution to arrive at the satndard contribution from actual sales given in the question. The total fixed costs variance, along with budgeted fixed costs, appears in a reconciliation statement below the actual contribution.

225 D

Ah × Ar =	$176,000		
		Rate variance	$36,000 A
Ah × Sr = 14,000 hrs × $10	$140,000		
		Efficiency variance	$25,000 F
Sh ×Sr = 3 hrs × 5,500 units × $10	$165,000		

226 D

Expenditure variance:

Monthly budgeted production (10,800/12) = 900 units

Monthly budgeted expenditure (Flexed budget)	$
Fixed costs (900 × $4)	3,600
Variable costs (800 × $6)	4,800
Total expected expenditure	8,400
Actual expenditure	8,500
Expenditure variance	100 (A)

114

Volume variance:

This only applies to fixed overhead costs:

Volume variance in units (900 – 800)	100 units (A)
Standard fixed overhead cost per unit	$4
Fixed overhead volume variance	$400 (A)

227 C

	$	
Expenditure variance	36,000	(A)
(= 10% of budgeted expenditure)		
Therefore budgeted expenditure 36,000/10 × 100	360,000	
	———	
Actual expenditure 36,000/10 × 110	396,000	
	———	

228 C

Fixed production overhead cost per unit = $120,000/20,000 units = $6 per unit.

Standard units ×	OAR	
21,000	$6	$126,000
Budget units ×	OAR	
20,000	$6	$120,000
	Volume variance	$6,000 F

229 A

Budgeted hours of work = 30,000 units × 4 hours = 120,000 hours.

Fixed overhead absorption rate/hour = $840,000/120,000 hours = $7/hour.

Actual hours ×	OAR	
123,000	$7	$861,000
Budget hours ×	OAR	
120,000	$7	$840,000
	Capacity variance	$21,000 F

230 C

Budgeted fixed overhead cost per unit = $48,000/4,800 units = $10.

	$	
Budgeted fixed overhead	48,000	
Expenditure variance	2,000	(A)
	———	
Actual fixed overhead	50,000	
	———	

	$
Actual fixed overhead	50,000
Under-absorbed fixed overhead	8,000
Absorbed overhead	42,000

Units produced = Absorbed overhead/Absorption rate per unit

= $42,000/$10 = 4,200 units.

231 C

This is a definition of 'basic standards'. Basic standards are not widely used in practice.

232 A

True is the correct answer because quality is of increasing importance. This means that materials are often bought on long-term contracts and a premium may be paid for quality. Staff may be multi-skilled and more experienced and therefore paid a higher wage rate. Management may be more concerned about the quality of the process than achieving standard costs.

233 C

Less experienced staff are likely to be paid at a lower rate and therefore the labour rate variance will be favourable.

Usage of materials is likely to be unfavourable as the staff are less experienced, thus there will be more wastage and a higher level of rejects.

234 D

Usage of materials is likely to be unfavourable as the materials are sub-standard, thus there will be more wastage and a higher level of rejects.

Time spent by the labour force on rejected items that will not become output leads to higher than standard time spent per unit of output.

235 A

Ah × Ar = 29,000 × **$3.80**	$110,200	
	Rate variance	$5,800 F
Ah × Sr = 29,000 × $4	$116,000	
	Efficiency variance	$4,000 F
Sh ×Sr = 30,000 × $4	$120,000	

236 D

Ah × Ar = 10,080 × $0.87	$8,770	
	Rate variance	$706 A
Ah × Sr = 10,080 × $0.80	$8,064	
	Efficiency variance	$256 F
Sh ×Sr = **2.08** × 5,000 × $0.80	$8,320	

237 C

Standard hours ×	OAR	
710 × 0.5	$12	$4,260
Actual hours ×	OAR	
378 - 20	$12	$4,296
	Efficiency variance	$36 A

238 C

Ah × Ar = 4,800 × $0.87	$7,700	
	Expenditure variance	$500 A
Ah × Sr = 4,800 × $1.50	$7,200	
	Efficiency variance	$300 F
Sh ×Sr = 500 ×10 × $1.50	$7,500	

239 B

(Budgeted quantity – Actual quantity) × standard profit per unit

(1,000 – 900) × ($50 – $39) = $1,100

240 A

Fixed overhead expenditure variance = Actual cost – Budgeted cost = $1,250 A	
Actual overhead	= Budgeted cost – 2%
2%	= $1,250
Actual overhead = 1,250 / 2 × 98	= $61,250

241 C

242 B

This statement is false because the sales volume variance under marginal costing is based on standard contribution per unit (whereas the sales volume variance under absorption costing is based on standard profit per unit).

243 D

See working below (244)

244 A

Aq × Ap =	$173,280	
	Price variance	**$9,120 F**
Aq × Sp = 45,600 ×$ 4	$182,400	
	Usage variance	$15,200 A
Sq ×Sp = **3,344 units** × 12.5kg × $4	$167,200	

245 B

The purchase of the new machine is likely to result in improved efficiency but higher depreciation costs.

246 D

	Standard hours ×	OAR	
	3,700 × 1.5	$2.40	$13,320
	Budget hours ×	OAR	
	4,000 ×1.5	$2.40	$14,400
		Volume variance	$1,080 A

247 C

(i)   will affect the sales price variance.

248 D

Aq × Sp = 1,566 × (76,500/1,500) $79,866
                                                            Usage variance $5,916 A
Sq ×Sp = (580 × 1,500/600) × (76,500/1,500) $73,950

249 D

Aq × Sp = **1,650** × $2 $3,300
                                        Usage variance $300 A
Sq ×Sp = 500 × 3kg × $2 $3,000

500 units did use	**1,650**
Less opening inventory	(100)
Plus closing inventory	400
Material purchases in kg	1,950

250 A

Aq × Ap = $23,839
                                                      Price variance $783 F
Aq × Sp = 1,566 × ($25,500/1500) $26,622

251 C

Expenditure variance = Budget cost – actual cost	= (8,000 × 15) – (8,500 × 17)
	= $24,500 A
Volume variance (8,500 – 8,000) × $15	= $7,500 F
Total variance	= $17,000 A

252 A

The standard contribution per unit is $(50 – 4 – 16 – 10 – 1) = $19.

Sales volume variance

= (Budgeted sales volume – actual sales volume) × Standard contribution per unit

= (3,000 – 3,500) × $19

= $9,500

253 C

Sales volume variance

= (Budgeted sales volume – actual sales volume) × Standard profit per unit

= (10,000 – 9,800) × $5

= $1,000 A

254 B

Actual hours ×	OAR	
5,500	$15	$82,500
Budget hours ×	OAR	
5,000	$15	$75,000
	Capacity variance	$7,500 F

255 B

Ah × Ar =		117,600	
		Rate variance	$8,400 A
Ah × Sr = 28,000 × **$3.90**		$109,200	
		Efficiency variance	$3,900 F
Sh ×Sr = **29,000** × $3.90		$113,100	

PERFORMANCE MEASUREMENT TECHNIQUES

256 B

Controllable assets = 80,000 ÷ 0.25 = $320,000

RI = $80,000 – ($320,000 × 0.18) = $80,000 – $57,600 = $22,400

257 C

Cost per patient is a measure of output related to input

258 A

259 B

Reducing mortality rates is likely to be a stated objective of the hospital and as such is a measure of output, or effectiveness

260 B

Contribution is calculated as sales revenue less variable costs. The manager of a cost centre will not be responsible for the revenue therefore this is not an appropriate measure.

261 C

Class sizes are the result of the number of pupils educated (output), the number of teachers employed (input) and how well the timetable is organised in using those teachers.

262 D

Measuring the budgeted number of quotations actually issued would be monitoring the output and activity of the department but it would not be helpful in improving the department's performance in terms of the accuracy or speed of quotations in the scenario described.

263 C

Revenue is most likely to be based on the quantity delivered and the distance travelled. Cost per tonne miles gives a measure of both quantity and distance

264 C

RI = Net profit before interest − (10% × invested capital)

Therefore £240,000 = £640,000 − (10% × invested capital)

So 10% × invested capital = £400,000

Therefore invested capital = £4m

$$\text{ROI} = \frac{\text{Net profit before interest}}{\text{Invested capital}} = \frac{£640,000}{£4,000,000} \times 100 = 16\%$$

265 B

The manager of a profit centre can exercise control over revenues and controllable costs, but has no influence concerning the capital invested in the centre.

Contribution (i) would be a useful performance measure because a profit centre manager can exercise control over sales revenue and variable costs. Controllable profit (ii) would also be useful. Return on investment (iii), residual income (iv) would not be useful because they require a measure of the capital invested in the division.

266 C

Actual output in standard hours = 1,100 × 2 = 2,200 hours

Budgeted production hours = 2,000 hours

Production /volume ratio = 2,200/2,000 = 1.1 or 110%

267 A

Actual output in standard hours = 180 × 0.6 = 108 hours

Actual production hours = 126 hours

Efficiency ratio = 108/126 = 0.857 or 86%

268 D

Actual production hours = 61 hours

Budgeted production hours = 50 × 1.2 = 60 hours

Capacity ratio = 61/60 = 1.017 or 102%

269 D

270 B

(i) and (ii) are financial indicators and (iv) is a risk indicator

271 C

272 B

273 D

274 A

275 C

SPREADSHEETS

276 C

A database contains records and files and is most suitable for storing large volumes of data

277 C

The formula for correlation is $r = \dfrac{n\sum xy - (\sum x)(\sum y)}{\sqrt{\{n\sum x^2 - (\sum x)^2\}\{n\sum y^2 - (\sum y)^2\}}}$

Here n is 7 and to construct the formula we need to identify the appropriate totals from row 11.

A and D are wrong because they use n = 6.

B is wrong because it lacks the square root required for the bottom of the formula.

278 B

All are said to be advantages of spreadsheet software with the exception of (i) security. A computer-based approach exposes the firm to threats from viruses, hackers and general system failure.

279 D

Budgeted production for a period = budgeted sales for the period –opening inventory of finished goods for the period + closing inventory of finished goods for the period.

Sales	F3
(Opening Inventory)	(10% F3)
Closing Inventory	10% F4
Production	90% F3 + 10% F4
	Or [(0.9*F3) + (0.1*F4)]

280 B

Using graphics is usually done using the chart wizard not the format cells option.

Section 3

PILOT PAPER EXAM QUESTIONS

1   A manufacturing company benchmarks the performance of its accounts receivable department with that of a leading credit card company.

What type of benchmarking is the company using?

A   Internal benchmarking

B   Competitive benchmarking

C   Functional benchmarking

D   Strategic benchmarking

2   **Which of the following BEST describes target costing?**

A   Setting a cost by subtracting a desired profit margin from a competitive market price

B   Setting a price by adding a desired profit margin to a production cost

C   Setting a cost for the use in the calculation of variances

D   Setting a selling price for the company to aim for in the long run

3   **Information relating to two processes (F and G) was as follows:**

Process	Normal loss as % of input	Input (litres)	Output (litres)
F	8	65,000	58,900
G	5	37,500	35,700

For each process, was there an abnormal loss or an abnormal gain?

	Process F	Process G
A	Abnormal gain	Abnormal gain
B	Abnormal gain	Abnormal loss
C	Abnormal loss	Abnormal gain
D	Abnormal loss	Abnormal loss

4   The following budgeted information relates to a manufacturing company for next period:

	Units		$
Production	14,000	Fixed production costs	63,000
Sales	12,000	Fixed selling costs	12,000

The normal level of activity is 14,000 units per period.

Using absorption costing the profit for next period has been calculated as $36,000.

What would be the profit for next period using marginal costing?

A $25,000

B $27,000

C $45,000

D $47,000

5   A company has a budgeted material cost of $125,000 for the production of 25,000 units per month. Each unit is budgeted to use 2 kg of material. The standard cost of material is $2·50 per kg. Actual materials in the month cost $136,000 for 27,000 units and 53,000 kg were purchased and used.

What was the adverse material price variance?

A $1,000

B $3,500

C $7,500

D $11,000

6   **Under which sampling method does every member of the target population have an equal chance of being in the sample?**

A   Stratified sampling

B   Random sampling

C   Systematic sampling

D   Cluster sampling

7   **The following statements refer to spreadsheets:**

(1)   A spreadsheet is the most suitable software for the storage of large volume of data

(2)   A spreadsheet could be used to produce a flexible budget

(3)   Most spreadsheets contain a facility to display the data within them in a graphical form

Which of these statements are correct?

A   1 and 2 only

B   1 and 3 only

C   2 and 3 only

D   1, 2 and 3

KAPLAN PUBLISHING

8   Up to a given level of activity in each period the purchase price per unit of a raw material is constant. After that point a lower price per unit applies both to further units purchased and also retrospectively to all units already purchased.

Which of the following graphs depicts the total cost of the raw materials for a period?

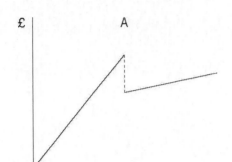

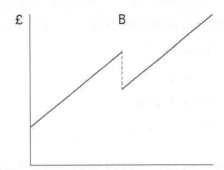

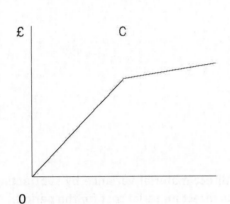

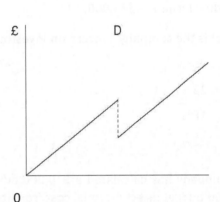

A   Graph A

B   Graph B

C   Graph C

D   Graph D

9   **Which of the following are benefits of budgeting?**

(1)   It helps coordinate the activities of different departments

(2)   It fulfils legal reporting obligations

(3)   It establishes a system of control

(4)   It is a starting point for strategic planning

A   (1) and (4) only

B   (1) and (3) only

C   (2) and (3) only

D   (2) and (4) only

10   The following statements relate to the participation of junior management in setting budgets:

(1)   It speeds up the setting of budgets

(2)   It increases the motivation of junior managers

(3)   It reduces the level of budget padding

Which statements are true?

A   (1) only

B   (2) only

C   (2) and (3) only

D   (1), (2) and (3)

11   A company has a capital employed of $200,000. It has a cost of capital of 12% per year. Its residual income is $36,000.

What is the company's return on investment?

A   30%

B   12%

C   18%

D   22%

12   A company has calculated a $10,000 adverse direct material variance by subtracting its flexed budget direct material cost from its actual direct material cost for the period.

Which of the following could have caused the variance?

(1)   An increase in direct material prices

(2)   An increase in raw material usage per unit

(3)   Units produced being greater than budgeted

(4)   Units sold being greater than budgeted

A   2 and 3 only

B   3 and 4 only

C   1 and 2 only

D   1 and 4 only

13   An organisation has the following total costs at two activity levels:

Activity level (units)	16,000	22,000
Total costs ($)	135,000	170,000

Variable costs per unit is constant within this range of activity but there is a step up of $5,000 in the total fixed costs when the activity exceeds 17,500 units.

What is the total cost at an activity level of 20,000 units?

A $163,320

B $158,320

C $160,000

D $154,545

14   **Which of the following are suitable measures of performance at the strategic level?**

(1)   Return on investment

(2)   Market share

(3)   Number of customer complaints

A   1 and 2

B   2 only

C   2 and 3

D   1 and 3

15   **Which of the following are feasible values for the correlation coefficient?**

(1)   +1·40

(2)   +1·04

(3)   0

(4)   −0·94

A   (1) and (2) only

B   (3) and (4) only

C   (1), 2) and (4) only

D   (1), (2), (3) and (4)

16   **A company's operating costs are 60% variable and 40% fixed.**

Which of the following variances' values would change if the company switched from standard marginal costing to standard absorption costing?

A   Direct material efficiency variance

B   Variable overhead efficiency variance

C   Sales volume variance

D   Fixed overhead expenditure variance

17   ABC Co has a manufacturing capacity of 10,000 units. The flexed production cost budget
     of the company is as follows:

Capacity   60%   100%

Total production costs $11,280 $15,120

What is the budgeted total production cost if it operates at 85% capacity?

A $13,680

B $12,852

C $14,025

D $12,340

18   Using an interest rate of 10% per year the net present value (NPV) of a project has been
     correctly calculated as $50. If the interest rate is increased by 1% the NPV of the project
     falls by $20.

What is the internal rate of return (IRR) of the project?

A   7·5%

B   11·7%

C   12·5%

D   20·0%

19   **Which of the following BEST describes a principle budget factor?**

A   A factor that affects all budget centres

B   A factor that is controllable by a budget centre manager

C   A factor that the management accountant builds into all budgets

D   A factor which limits the activities of an organisation

20   A company always determines its order quantity for a raw material by using the Economic
     Order Quantity (EOQ) model.

**What would be the effects on the EOQ and the total annual holding cost of a decrease in
the cost of ordering a batch of raw material?**

	EOQ	Annual holding cost
A	Higher	Lower
B	Higher	Higher
C	Lower	Higher
D	Lower	Lower

21 A company which operates a process costing system had work-in-progress at the start of last month of 300 units (valued at $1,710) which were 60% complete in respect of all costs. Last month a total of 2,000 units were completed and transferred to the finished goods warehouse. The cost per equivalent unit for costs arising last month was $10. The company uses the FIFO method of cost allocation.

What was the total value of the 2,000 units transferred to the finished goods warehouse last month?

A $19,910

B $20,000

C $20,510

D $21,710

22 A manufacturing company operates a standard absorption costing system. Last month 25,000 production hours were budgeted and the budgeted fixed production cost was $125,000. Last month the actual hours worked were 24,000 and standard hours for actual production were 27,000.

What was the fixed production overhead capacity variance for last month?

A $5,000 Adverse

B $5,000 Favourable

C $10,000 Adverse

D $10,000 Favourable

23 The following statements have been made about value analysis.

(1)   It seeks the lowest cost method of achieving a desired function

(2)   It always results in inferior products

(3)   It ignores esteem value

(4)   It is applicable to both physical products and services

Which TWO of the above statements are true?

A   (1 and 4

B   (1 and 2

C   3 and 4

D   2 and 3

24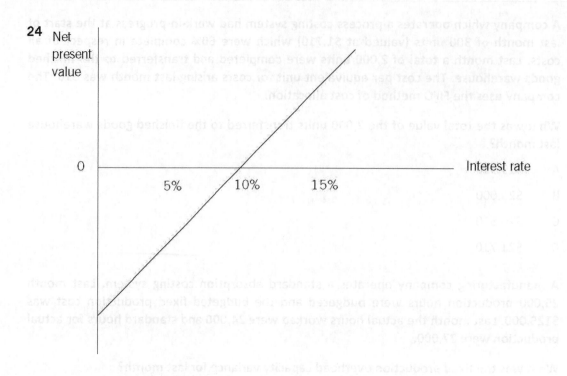

Which of the following is correct with regard to the above graph?

(1)   The IRR is 10%

(2)   The NPV at 15% is positive

(3)   The project's total inflows exceed the total outflows

A   (1) and (2) only

B   (1) and (3) only

C   (2) and (3) only

D   (1), (2) and (3)

25   A company uses standard absorption costing. The following data relate to last month:

	Budget	Actual
Sales and production (units)	1,000	900
	Standard ($)	Actual ($)
Selling price per unit	50	52
Total production cost per unit	39	40

What was the adverse sales volume profit variance last month?

A $1,000

B $1,100

C $1,200

D $1,300

26   The following statements relate to the advantages that linear regression analysis has over the high low method in the analysis of cost behaviour:

(1)   the reliability of the analysis can be statistically tested

(2)   it takes into account all of the data

(2)   it assumes linear cost behaviour

Which statements are true?

A   (1) only

B   (1) and (2) only

C   (2) and (3) only

D   (1), (2) and (3)

27   **Mr Manaton has recently won a competition where he has the choice between receiving $5,000 now or an annual amount forever starting now (i.e. a level perpetuity starting immediately). The interest rate is 8% per annum.**

What would be the value of the annual perpetuity to the nearest $?

A $370

B $500

C $400

D $620

28   **Which of the following would not be expected to appear in an organisation's mission statement?**

A   The organisation's values and beliefs

B   The products or services offered by the organisation

C   Quantified short term targets the organisation seeks to achieve

D   The organisation's major stakeholders

29   **An organisation operates a piecework system of remuneration, but also guarantees its employees 80% of a time-based rate of pay which is based on $20 per hour for an eight hour working day. Three minutes is the standard time allowed per unit of output. Piecework is paid at the rate of $18 per standard hour.**

If an employee produces 200 units in eight hours on a particular day, what is the employee's gross pay for that day?

A $128

B $144

C $160

D $180

30 A company uses an overhead absorption rate of $3·50 per machine hour, based on 32,000 budgeted machine hours for the period. During the same period the actual total overhead expenditure amounted to $108,875 and 30,000 machine hours were recorded on actual production.

By how much was the total overhead under or over absorbed for the period?

A   Under absorbed by $3,875

B   Under absorbed by $7,000

C   Over absorbed by $3,875

D   Over absorbed by $7,000

31 **Which of the following statements relating to management information are true?**

(1)   It is produced for parties external to the organisation

(2)   There is usually a legal requirement for the information to be produced

(3)   No strict rules govern the way in which the information is presented

(4)   It may be presented in monetary or non monetary terms

A   (1) and (2)

B   (3) and (4)

C   (1) and (3)

D   (2) and (4)

32 **A company's sales in the last year in its three different markets were as follows**

	$
Market 1	100,000
Market 2	150,000
Market 3	50,000
	Total 300,000

In a pie chart representing the proportion of sales made by each region what would be the angle of the section representing Market 3?

A   17 degrees

B   50 degrees

C   60 degrees

D   120 degrees

33 **Which of the following BEST describes a flexible budget?**

A   A budget which shows variable production costs only

B   A monthly budget which is changed to reflect the number of days in the month

C   A budget which shows sales revenue and costs at different levels of activity

D   A budget that is updated halfway through the year to incorporate the actual results for the first half of the year

34 **The Eastland Postal Service is government owned. The government requires it to provide a parcel delivery service to every home and business in Eastland at a low price which is set by the government. Express Couriers Co is a privately owned parcel delivery company that also operates in Eastland. It is not subject to government regulation and most of its deliveries are to large businesses located in Eastland's capital city. You have been asked to assess the relative efficiency of the management of the two organisations.**

Which of the following factors should NOT be allowed for when comparing the ROCE of the two organisations to assess the efficiency of their management?

A   Differences in prices charged

B   Differences in objectives pursued

C   Differences in workforce motivation

D   Differences in geographic areas served

35 **Two products G and H are created from a joint process. G can be sold immediately after split-off. H requires further processing into product HH before it is in a saleable condition. There are no opening inventories and no work in progress of products G, H or HH. The following data are available for last period:**

	$
Total joint production costs	350,000
Further processing costs of product H	66,000

Product	Production units	Closing inventory
G	420,000	20,000
HH	330,000	30,000

Using the physical unit method for apportioning joint production costs, what was the cost value of the closing inventory of product HH for last period?

A $16,640

B $18,625

C $20,000

D $21,600

36   **Which TWO of the following are true for flexible budgets?**

(1)   A budget which is continually updated to reflect actual results

(2)   A budget which has built in contingency to allow for unforeseen events

(3)   A budget which identifies the cost behaviour of different cost items

(4)   A budget which allows comparison of like with like

A   (1) and (2)

B   (1) and (4)

C   (2) and (3)

D   (3) and (4)

37   **A company manufactures and sells a single product. In two consecutive months the following levels of production and sales (in units) occurred:**

	Month 1	Month 2
Sales	3,800	4,400
Production	3,900	4,200

The opening inventory for Month 1 was 400 units. Profits or losses have been calculated for each month using both absorption and marginal costing principles.

Which of the following combination of profits and losses for the two months is consistent with the above data?

	Absorption costing profit/(loss)		Marginal costing profit/(loss)	
	Month 1	Month 2	Month 1	Month 2
	$	$	$	$
A	200	4,400	(400)	3,200
B	(400)	4,400	200	3,200
C	200	3,200	(400)	4,400
D	(400)	3,200	200	4,400

38   **A company wishes to evaluate a division which has the following extracts from income statement and statement of financial position.**

Income statement:

	$'000
Sales	500
Gross profit	200
Net profit	120

Statement of financial position:

	$'000
Non-current assets	750
Current assets	350
Current liabilities	(450)
Net assets	650

What is the residual income for the division if the company has a cost of capital of 18%?

A $117,000

B $21,600

C $83,000

D $3,000

39   Under which of the following labour remuneration methods will direct labour cost always be a variable cost?

A   Day rate

B   Piece rate

C   Differential piece rate

D   Group bonus scheme

40   A firm uses marginal costing. The following table shows the variances for a period when the actual net profit was $30,000.

Materials	$300 adverse
Labour	$800 favourable
Overheads	$550 adverse
Sales price variance	$400 favourable
Sales volume contribution variance	$800 favourable

What was the budgeted net profit for the period?

A $28,850

B $31,150

C $30,050

D $28,800

41   The use of the balanced scorecard rather than a profit-based measure is likely to help solve the following problems:

(1)   Subjectivity

(2)   Short-termism

Which is/are true?

A   (1) only

B   (2) only

C   Both (1) and (2)

D   Neither (1) nor (2)

42 A company operates a process in which no losses are incurred. The process account for last month, when there was no opening work-in-progress, was as follows:

Process Account

	$		$
Costs arising	624,000	Finished output (10,000 units)	480,000
		Closing work-in-progress (4,000 units)	144,000
	624,000		624,000

The closing work in progress was complete to the same degree for all elements of cost.

What was the percentage degree of completion of the closing work-in-progress?

A   12%

B   30%

C   40%

D   75%

43 The purchase price of an item of inventory is $25 per unit. In each three month period the usage of the item is 20,000 units. The annual holding costs associated with one unit equate to 6% of its purchase price. The cost of placing an order for the item is $20.

What is the Economic Order Quantity (EOQ) for the inventory item to the nearest whole unit?

A   730

B   894

C   1,461

D   1,633

44 A factory consists of two production cost centres (P and Q) and two service cost centres (X and Y). The total allocated and apportioned overhead for each is as follows:

P	Q	X	Y
$95,000	$82,000	$46,000	$30,000

It has been estimated that each service cost centre does work for other cost centres in the following proportions:

	P	Q	X	Y
Percentage of service cost centre X to	50	50	–	–
Percentage of service cost centre Y to	30	60	10	–

The reapportionment of service cost centre costs to other cost centres fully reflects the above proportions.

After the reapportionment of service cost centre costs has been carried out, what is the total overhead for production cost centre P?

A $124,500

B $126,100

C $127,000

D $128,500

45   The following statements relate to responsibility centres:

(1)   Return on capital employed is a suitable measure of performance in both profit and investment centres.

(2)   Cost centres are found in manufacturing organisations but not in service organisations.

(3)   The manager of a revenue centre is responsible for both sales and costs in a part of an organisation.

Which of the statements, if any, is true?

A   (1) only

B   (2) only

C   (3) only

D   None of them

46   A company has recorded the following variances for a period:

Sales volume variance $10,000 adverse

Sales price variance $5,000 favourable

Total cost variance $12,000 adverse

Standard profit on actual sales for the period was $120,000.

What was the fixed budget profit for the period?

A $137,000

B $103,000

C $110,000

D $130,000

47   A Company manufactures and sells one product which requires 8 kg of raw material in its manufacture. The budgeted data relating to the next period are as follows:

	Units
Sales	19,000
Opening inventory of finished goods	4,000
Closing inventory of finished goods	3,000

	Kg
Opening inventory of raw materials	50,000
Closing inventory of raw materials	53,000

What is the budgeted raw material purchases for next period (in kg)?

A   141,000

B   147,000

C   157,000

D   163,000

48 The following statements relate to performance evaluation methods:

(1) Residual income is not a relative measure

(2) The return on investment figure is a relative measure

(3) Residual income cannot be calculated for an individual project

Which of the above are correct?

A (1) and (2) only

B (1) and (3) only

C (2) and (3) only

D (1), (2) and (3)

49 A company has a budget for two products A and B as follows:

	Product A	Product B
Sales (units)	2,000	4,500
Production (units)	1,750	5,000
Skilled labour at $10/hour	2 hours/unit	2 hours/unit
Unskilled labour at $7/hour	3 hours/unit	4 hours/unit

What is the budgeted cost of unskilled labour for the period?

A $105,000

B $135,000

C $176,750

D $252,500

50 Which TWO of the following are MOST likely to influence the motivation of budget holders?

(1) The contents of the budget manual

(2) The extent of participation in budget setting

(3) The level of difficulty at which budgets are set

(4) The structure of the budget committee

A (1) and (2)

B (2) and (3)

C (3) and (4)

D (1) and (4)

Section 4

ANSWERS TO PILOT PAPER EXAM QUESTIONS

1   C

2   A

3   C

	Normal loss	Actual loss	Abnormal loss	Abnormal gain
Process F	5,200	6,100	900	–
Process G	1,875	1,800	–	75

4   B

Marginal costing profit:

$(36,000 - (2,000 \times (63,000/14,000))) = \$27,000$

5   B

Did cost:	$136,000
Should cost (53,000 kg × $2.50)	$132,500
Price variance	$3,500

6   B

7   C

8   D

9   B

10   B

11   A

$(36,000 + (200,000 \times 12\%))/200,000 = 30\%$

12 **C**

13 **C**

Using the high low method:

Variable cost:

($170,000 – $5,000 – $135,000)/(22,000 – 16,000) = $5

Fixed cost:

135,000 – (16,000 × 5) = $55,000

Cost for 20,000 units:

(20,000 × 5) + (55,000 + 5,000) = $160,000

14 **A**

15 **B**

16 **C**

17 **A**

Variable production cost per unit:

($15,120 – $11,280)/(10,000– 6,000) = $3,840/4,000 = $0·96

Fixed cost = $11,280 – (6,000 × 0·96) = $5,520

85% capacity = 8,500 units.

Flexible budget allowance for 8,500 units:

$5,520 + (8,500 × 0·96) = $13,680

18 **C**

At 11% NPV should be $20

Using interpolation: 10 +[(50/(50 - 30)](11 – 10) = 12·5%

19 **D**

20 **D**

21 **A**

1,700 units × 10	$17,000
300 units × 0·4 × 10	$1,200
Opening work in progress value	$1,710
Total value	$19,910

22 **A**

(Actual hours – Budgeted hours) × standard rate

(24,000 – 25,000) × $5 = $5,000 adverse

23 A

24 A

25 B

(budgeted quantity – actual quantity) × standard profit per unit

(1,000 – 900) × ($50 – $39) = $1,100

26 B

27 A

$5,000 = x + x/0.08$

$5,000 = 13.5x$

Value of annual perpetuity = 5,000/13.5 = $370

28 C

29 D

200 units × (3/60) × $18 = $180

30 A

Actual cost	$108,875
Absorbed cost	$105,000
Under absorbed	$3,875

31 B

32 C

Total number of degrees = 360°

Proportion of market 3 sales: (50,000/300,000) × 360° = 60°

33 C

34 C

35   C

Joint costs apportioned to H: ((330,000/(420,000 + 330,000)) × $350,000 = $154,000

Closing inventory valuation(HH): (30,000/330,000) × ($154,000 + $66,000) = $20,000

36   D

37   C

Month 1: production >sales   Absorption costing > marginal costing

Month 2: sales> production   Marginal costing profit> absorption costing profit

A and C satisfy month 1, C and D satisfy month 2; therefore C satisfies both

38   D

($120,000 − ($650,000 × 18%) = $3,000

39   B

40   A

($30,000 + $300 − $800 + $550 − $400 − $800) = $28,850

41   B

42   D

Cost per equivalent unit (480,000/10,000) = $48

Degree of completion= ((144,000/48)/4,000) = 75%

43   C

$$\{(2 \times 20 \times (4 \times 20,000))/(0{\cdot}06 \times 25)\}^{0{\cdot}5}$$
1,461 units

44   D

Direct cost	$95,000
Proportion of cost centre X ($46,000 + (0·10 × $30,000)) × 0·50	$24,500
Proportion of cost centre Y ($30,000 × 0·3)	$9,000
Total overhead cost for P	$128,500

45   D

46 D

Sales volume variance:

(budgeted sales units – actual sales units) × standard profit per unit = $10,000 adverse

Standard profit on actual sales: (actual sales units × std profit per unit) = $120,000

Fixed budget profit: ($120,000 + $10,000) = $130,000

47 B

Budgeted production (19,000 + 3,000 – 4,000) = 18,000 units

RM required for production (18,000 × 8) = 144,000 kg

RM purchases (144,000 + 53,000 – 50,000) = 147,000 kg

48 A

49 C

(($1,750 × 3 hrs) + ($5,000 × 4 hrs)) × 7 = $176,750

50 B

Section 5

PRACTICE SIMULATION QUESTIONS

ALL QUESTIONS ARE WORTH 2 MARKS

QUESTION 1

The following details are available for a company:

	Budgeted	Actual
Expenditure	£176,400	£250,400
Machine hours	4,000	5,000
Labour hours	3,600	5,400

If the company absorbs overheads using labour hours, then, during the period, overheads were:

A   Under-absorbed by £29,900

B   Under-absorbed by £14,200

C   Over-absorbed by £14,200

D   Over-absorbed by £64,990

QUESTION 2

A company uses process costing in calculating output cost. The following details are available for a particular department in December 20X8. All materials are added at the start of the process:

Opening Work in Progress	Nil Units
Units started	10,000 units
Closing Work-in-Progress	1,000 units
	100% complete for materials
	75% complete for conversion
Normal loss	200 units
Units completed	8,000 units

If all losses occur at the start of the process, how many equivalent units should be included for materials?

A   7,750

B   8,750

C   8,800

D   9,800

QUESTION 3

A principal budget factor is a factor common to all functions in budget preparation.

A   True

B   False

QUESTION 4

A random sample is defined as a sample taken in such a way that every member of the population has an equal chance of being selected.

A   True

B   False

QUESTION 5

A sunk cost is a relevant cost.

Is this statement true or false?

A   True

B   False

QUESTION 6

The following data is available for a company in period 2.

Actual overheads $225,900
Actual machine hours   7,530
Budgeted overheads $216,000

Based on the data above and assuming that the budgeted overhead absorption rate was $32 per hour, the number of machine hours (to the nearest hour) that were budgeted to be worked were:

A   7,059

B   6,750

C   6,900

D   7,000

QUESTION 7

Overhead absorption is a means of attributing total costs to a cost unit.

A   True

B   False

QUESTION 8

The following table shows that the typical salary of part qualified accountants in five different regions of England.

Area	Typical salary
	£
South-east	21,500
Midlands	20,800
North-east	18,200
North-west	17,500
South-west	16,700

The best diagram to draw to highlight the differences between areas is:

A   a pie diagram

B   a multiple bar chart

C   a percentage component bar chart

D   a simple bar chart

QUESTION 9

In times of decreasing prices, the valuation of inventory using the First In First Out method, as opposed to the Weighted Average Cost method, will result in which ONE of the following combinations?

	Cost of sales	Profit	Closing inventory
A	Lower	Higher	Higher
B	Lower	Higher	Lower
C	Higher	Lower	Lower
D	Higher	Higher	Lower

QUESTION 10

A manufacturing company uses 28,000 components at an even rate during the year. Each order placed with the supplier of the components is for 1,600 components, which is the Economic Order Quantity. The company holds a buffer inventory of 800 components. The annual cost of holding one component in inventory is €3.50.

What is the Annual Cost of holding inventory of the component?

A   €2,800

B   €4,200

C   €5,600

D   €5,700

The following data relates to Questions 11 and 12.

Normal working week	36 hours
Basic rate of pay (direct)	$6.20 per hour
Overtime pay	$7.50 per hour

Last week, the total hours worked by all these workers was 936. The overtime hours worked was 108. All employees worked at least their basic 36 hours.

QUESTION 11

The number of workers who worked last week:

A   was 23

B   was 26

C   was 29

D   cannot be determined from the above data

QUESTION 12

The total direct labour charge for the above was:

A $810.00

B $5,133.60

C $5,803.20

D $6,210.00

QUESTION 13

Your firm values inventory using the weighted average cost method. At 1 October 20X9, there were 50 units in inventory valued at $15 each. On 8 October, 30 units were purchased for $20 each, and a further 40 units were purchased for $17 each on 14 October. On 21 October, 60 units were sold for $1,800.

The value of closing inventory at 31 October 20X9 was:

A $230

B $950

C $1,015

D $1,125

QUESTION 14

Service costing is characterised by high levels of indirect costs as a proportion of total costs and the use of composite cost units.

A   True

B   False

QUESTION 15

A Company has four departments – Assembly, Finishing, Maintenance and Administration. Budgeted data for each department is shown below:

	Assembly	Finishing	Maintenance
Allocated overheads	$90,000	$100,000	$10,000
Direct labour hours	5,000	6,000	Nil
Machine hours	10,000	3,000	2,000
Percentage of time spent maintaining machinery	60	40	Nil
Number of staff	60	120	10

The most appropriate production overhead absorption rate to use in the Assembly department would be:

A   £9.60 per machine hour

B   £9.90 per machine hour

C   £17.33 per labour hour

D   £18.33 per labour hour

QUESTION 16

Products A and B are manufactured in a joint process. The following data is available for a period:

Joint process costs		$30,000
Output:	Product A	2,000 kg
	Product B	4,000 kg
Selling price:	Product A	$12 per kg
	Product B	$18 per kg

What is Product B's share of the joint process costs if the sales value method of cost apportionment is used?

A   7,500

B   18,000

C   20,000

D   22,500

The following data relates to Questions 17 and 18.

Budgeted production details for November are as follows:

	Product X	Product Y	Product Z
Units produced	2,000	1,600	2,200
Units sold	1,800	1,500	2,000
Variable cost/unit	100	80	120
Fixed overhead absorbed/unit	30	30	50
No. of labour hours	6	4.5	5

There was no opening stock at the beginning of November.

QUESTION 17

Budgeted fixed overheads for November were:

A $810,000

B $739,000

C $218,000

D $199,000

QUESTION 18

Which of the following statements is true?

A   Absorption costing profit will be $19,000 lower than marginal costing profit

B   Absorption costing profit will be $71,000 lower than marginal costing profit

C   Absorption costing profit will be $19,000 higher than marginal costing profit

D   Absorption costing profit will be $71,000 higher than marginal costing profit

QUESTION 19

The total costs incurred at various output levels in a factory have been measured as follows:

Output in units	Total cost
25	£5,500
30	£5,450
33	£5,550
44	£6,000
48	£6,500
52	£7,000

The variable cost per unit and the Total Fixed Costs are (rounded figures):

A   Variable Cost £50 per unit, Fixed costs £4,000

B   Variable Cost £53 per unit, Fixed costs £4,000

C   Variable Cost £56 per unit, Fixed costs £4,111

D   Variable Cost £59 per unit, Fixed costs £4,111

QUESTION 20

A company makes a product that uses two materials. Standard cost information is given below:

Material A: 2 kg × $7

Material B: 3 litres × $11

In a period 1,300 units were made, and the following actual results were recorded:

Material A: 2,600 kg were bought at a cost of $18,400 and 2,400 kg were used

Material B: 3,900 litres were bought at a cost of $38,800 and 4,000 litres were used.

The company maintains its stocks at standard cost.

What was the total price variance reported in the period?

A   4,300 (F)

B   3,600 (F)

C   3,900 (F)

D   3,600 (A)

QUESTION 21

Regression analysis is being used to find the line of best fit (y=a + bx) from eleven pairs of data. The calculations have produced the following information:

$\sum x$ 440
$\sum y$ 330
$\sum x^2$ 17,986
$\sum y^2$ 10,366
$\sum xy$ 13,467

And b = 0.69171

What the value of 'a' in the equation for the line of best fit?

A   0.63

B   0.69

C   2.33

D   5.33

QUESTION 22

Which of the following statements IS true when applied to fixed costs:

A   overhead costs are always fixed costs

B   as production levels increase, fixed cost per unit decreases

C   fixed costs are always irrelevant in a decision making situation

D   as the level of activity changes, fixed costs will also change

QUESTION 23

A job is budgeted to require 3,300 productive hours after incurring 25% idle time. If the total labour cost budgeted for the job is $36,300, what is the labour cost per hour (to the nearest penny)?

A $8.25

B $8.80

C $11.00

D $13.75

QUESTION 24

Which of the following statement about variable costs is correct?

Variable costs are conventionally deemed to:

A   be constant per unit of output

B   vary per unit of output as production volume changes

C   vary in total when production volume is constant

D   vary, in total, from period to period when production is constant

QUESTION 25

In quality related costs, conformance costs include which of the following:

(i)   Internal failure costs

(ii)   Prevention costs

(iii)   Appraisal costs

(iv)   External failure costs

A   (i) and (ii)

B   (ii) and (iii)

C   (i), (ii) and (iii)

D   All of the above

QUESTION 26

A business is preparing its budget for the coming year by using time series analysis. Using the following information and a 3-month moving average what is the seasonal variation for the month of October?

Month	Sales value (000s)
June	770
July	750
August	928
September	854
October	834
November	1012
December	938

A   −66

B   −38

C   +66

D   +38

QUESTION 27

D Ltd operates a total absorption costing system. Budgeted fixed overheads for 2007 were $175,000 and budgeted production was 5,000 units.

During 2007, the actual fixed overheads amounted to $186,000 and actual production was 6,000 units. Overheads have been:

A   under-absorbed by $24,000

B   under-absorbed by $11,000

C   over-absorbed by $11,000

D   over-absorbed by $24,000

QUESTION 28

A continuous budget is prepared retrospectively.

Is this statement true or false?

A   True

B   False

QUESTION 29

Below is the standard cost card for one unit of product K.

	$/unit
Selling price	35
Direct materials	20
Direct labour	4
Variable overhead	1
Fixed overhead	6

Production was 50,000 units and sales 60,000 units. Opening inventory was 25,000 units. The profit calculated using marginal costing was $180,000. The profit using absorption costing is:

A $30,000

B $120,000

C $210,000

D $240,000

QUESTION 30

Direct costs are costs that:

A   can be directly identified with a product or service

B   are directly under the control of a manager

C   are incurred directly the factory is opened

D   are directly charged to a department

QUESTION 31

A company uses an industry wage rate index to forecast monthly wage costs. Employees receive a pay rise in September each year. The current monthly cost is £7,800 was calculated when the wage index was 134. The forecast wage rate index for the next three months is:

August	152
September	162
October	168

What will the wage cost be for September, to the nearest £?

A   £6,452

B   £6,876

C   £9,430

D   £8,848

QUESTION 32

A cost pool in ABC costing is an activity that consumes resources and for which overhead costs are identified and allocated.

A   True

B   False

QUESTION 33

A centre which is responsible for managing both costs and revenues is best described as:

A   Revenue centre

B   Investment centre

C   Profit centre

QUESTION 34

Pamper Pouches is considering an investment of $80,000 which will earn a contribution of $18,000 each year for 8 years at today's prices. The company's cost of capital is 10% per annum.

Calculate the net present value of the project.

A   ($40,780)

B   ($16,030)

C $40,780

D $16,030

QUESTION 35

Using an interest rate of 15% per year the net present value (NPV) of a project has been correctly calculated as $850.

If the interest rate is increased by 5% the NPV of the project falls by $900.

What is the internal rate of return (IRR) of the project?

A   14.7%

B   17.4%

C   19·7%

D   20·3%

QUESTION 36

The use of composite cost units is a characteristic of service costing.

A   True

B   False

The following data relates to questions 37 and 38

A company wishes to evaluate a division which has the following extracts from income statement and statement of financial position.

Income statement:

	$000
Sales	600
Gross profit	240
Net profit	144

Statement of financial position:

	$000
Non-current assets	750
Current assets	420
Current liabilities	(540)
Net assets	630

QUESTION 37

What is the gross profit percentage?

A   24%

B   40%

C   70%

D   90%

QUESTION 38

What is the current ratio?

A   0.56

B   0.67

C   0.78

D   1.28

QUESTION 39

Using data from 40 counties in England and Wales, it has been calculated that the correlation between the level of trampoline ownership and the number of neck injuries is 0.75. Which of the statements shown follow this?

(i)   High levels of trampoline ownership in a given county cause high levels of neck injuries.

(ii)   There is a strong relationship between the level of trampoline ownership and the number of neck injuries.

(iii)   56% of the variation in the level of neck injuries from one county to the next can be explained by the corresponding variation in the level of trampoline ownership.

(iv)   75% of the variation in the level of neck injuries from one county to the next can be explained by the corresponding variation in the level of trampoline ownership.

A   (i) and (ii) only

B   (i) and (iii) only

C   (ii) and (iii) only

D   (ii) and (iv) only

QUESTION 40

The Widget has a standard labour time of two hours per unit. The standard labour rate is $6 per hour. During one particular month 5,000 units were produced. The actual labour cost was $52,525 for 9,550 hours worked.

The labour rate variance is:

A $4,775 A

B $4,775 F

C $7,475 F

D $7,475 A

QUESTION 41

A company produces two types of Garden sheds, the Traditional and the Modern, which require 10 and 16 labour hours respectively. The budgeted data for the next period is as follows:

	Traditional	Modern
Sales	7,500	12,000
Opening inventory of finished goods	1,800	2,400

Closing inventory of finished goods are expected to be reduced by 50%.

What are the total budgeted labour hours for the next period?

A   295,200

B   267,000

C   238,800

D   210,600

QUESTION 42

The following statements refer to spreadsheets:

(1)   Spreadsheets can be used for budgeting.

(2)   Spreadsheets are very useful for word-processing.

(3)   Spreadsheets make the manipulation of data easier and quicker.

Which of these statements are correct?

A   (1) and (2)

B   (1) and (3)

C   (2) and (3)

D   (1), (2) and (3)

QUESTION 43

A company uses standard marginal costing. Last month, when all sales were at the standard selling price, the standard contribution from actual sales was $50,000 and the following variances arose:

Total variable costs variance	$3,500 adverse
Total fixed costs variance	$1,000 favourable
Sales volume contribution variance	$2,000 favourable

What was the actual contribution for last month?

A $46,500

B $47,500

C $48,500

D $49,500

QUESTION 44

A production worker is paid a salary of $650 per month, plus an extra 5 cents for each unit produced during the month. This labour cost is best described as:

A   A variable cost

B   A fixed cost

C   A step cost

D   A semi-variable cost

QUESTION 45

A supplier of telephone services charges a fixed line rental per period. The first 10 hours of telephone calls by the customer are free, after that all calls are charged at a constant rate per minute up to a maximum, thereafter all calls in the period are again free.

Which of the following graphs depicts the total cost to the customer of the telephone services in a period?

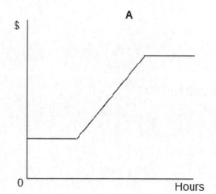

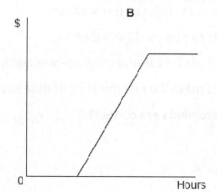

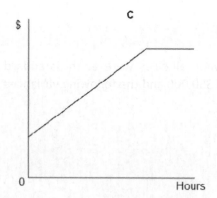

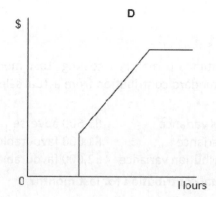

The following data relates to questions 46 and 47

A company wishes to evaluate a division which has the following extracts from income statement and statement of financial position.

Income statement:

	$'000
Sales	600
Gross profit	240
Net profit	144

Statement of financial position:

	$'000
Non-current assets	750
Current assets	420
Current liabilities	(540)
Net assets	630

QUESTION 46

What is the company's return on investment?

A   19%

B   22%

C   32%

D   38%

QUESTION 47

If the company's cost of capital is 12% what is the residual income?

A $68,400

B $93,600

C $164,400

D $189,600

The following information relates to questions 48 and 49.

During the month of December, a manufacturing process incurs material costs of £8,000 and conversion costs of £4,500. 2,000 kgs of material was input. There is a normal loss of 10% and all losses have a scrap value of £1.75 per kg. During the period, 1700 kgs were output to finished goods. Opening and Closing stocks in the process were nil.

QUESTION 48

The cost per kg output was:

A   £6.25

B   £6.75

C   £6.94

D   £7.35

QUESTION 49

The value of the abnormal loss written off in the profit and loss account will be

A   £675

B   £175

C   £2025

D   £500

QUESTION 50

Jojo is an assembly worker earning $12 per hour for a basic 35 hour week. Any overtime is paid at a premium of 50%.

In the last four-week period, Jojo was paid for 150 hours. During this time 15 hours were classed as idle due to a machine breaking down. Also included in the number of hours are four hours' overtime spent working for an urgent job at the request of the customer.

How much should be charged to the production overhead account for the four-week period?

A $216

B $240

C $288

D $360

Section 6

ANSWERS TO PRACTICE SIMULATION QUESTIONS

1   C

OAR = $176,400/3,600 = $49

		$
Amount absorbed = $49 × 5,400 =		264,600
Actual overhead		(250,400)
Over absorbed		14,200

2   D

Process account

	Units		Units
Materials (100% complete)	10,000	CWIP	1,000
		Normal loss	200
		Output	8,000
		Abnormal loss	800
	10,000		10,000

3   B – FALSE

A principal budget factor is a factor which limits the activities of the organisation.

4   A - TRUE

5   B

6   B

Budgeted hours = $\dfrac{\$216,000}{\$32}$ = 6,750 hours

7   B – FALSE

It is a method of attributing total production cost centre overheads to a cost unit, not total costs.

8 D

A simple bar chart would show five bars illustrating the different salaries in different regions.

9 C

When prices are decreasing, FIFO will give a lower valuation for closing inventory, because the closing inventory will consist of the most recently-purchased items. Lower closing inventory means higher cost of sales and lower profit.

10 C

{[Buffer inventory + (EOQ ÷ 2)] × Annual holding cost per component}

= [800 units + (1,600 units ÷ 2)] × €3.50 = €5,600

11 A

Normal time = 936 – 108 = 828 hours

Number of employees = 23

12 C

Direct labour charge is **all** hours (including overtime) at normal rate: 936 × $6.20 = $5,803.20

13 C

Date		Units	Unit value $	Inventory value $
1 October	Opening inventory	50		750
8 October	Purchase 30 units at $20	30		600
14 October	Purchase 40 units at $17	40		680
		120	16.92	2,030
21 October	Sold 75 units: cost	(60)	16.92	(1,015)
31 October	Closing inventory	60	16.92	1,015

14 A

15 A

	Assembly	Finishing	Maintenance
Allocated o/hs	90,000	100,000	10,000
Maintenance	6,000	4,000	(10,000)
	96,000	104,000	–

OAR for Assembly department = £96,000/10,000 machine hours = £9.60

16   D

	Output(kg)	Sales value ($)	Apportionment of joint costs ($)
Product A	2,000	24,000	(24/96) 7,500
Product B	4,000	72,000	(72/96) 22,500
		96,000	30,000

17   C

($30 × 2,000) + ($30 × 1,600) + ($50 × 2,200) = $218,000

18   C

All stocks are increasing, so absorption costing profits will be higher by:

($30 × 2,00) + ($30 × 100) + ($50 × 200) = $19,000

19   C

	Units	Total costs
High	52	£7,000
Low	25	£5,500
Difference	27	£1,500

Therefore, Variable costs = $\dfrac{£1,500}{27 \text{ units}}$ =£55.56 per unit

By substitution, we find FC = £4,111.

20   C

21   C

Y = a + bx

330/11 = a + (0.69171 × 440)/11

30 = a +27.66 so a = 2.33

22   B

23   A

Total hours worked, and paid = 3,300/0.75 = 4,400 hours

Hourly rate = $36,300/4,400 = $8.25

24   A

25   B

26 A

834 – [(854+834+1012)/3]=-66

27 D

Overheads incurred	186,000
Actual absorption $\dfrac{175,000}{5,000} \times 6,000$	210,000
	————
Over-absorbed	24,000

28 B

29 B

Marginal costing profit	180,000
Plus	
(15,000 – 25,000) × $6	(60,000)
	————
Equals absorption costing profit	120,000
	————

30 A

31 C

7,800/134 × 162 = £9,430

32 A - TRUE

33 C

34 D

Year	Cash flow	Discount factor	Present Value
0	(80,000)	1.000	(80,000)
1-10	18,000	5.335	96,030
NPV			**16,030**

35 C

15 + [850/(850+50)] × (20-15) = 19.7%

36 A

37 B

240/600 × 100 = 40%

38 C

420/540 = 0.78

39 C

40 B

AH × AR   = 9,550 × $5.5 = 52,525

Rate variance   **4,775 F**

AH × SR   = 9,550 × $6.0 = 57,300

41 C

Budgeted production

Traditional	= 7,500 + 900 – 1,800	= 6,600
Modern	= 12,000 + 1,200 – 2,400	= 10,800
Labour hours	= (6,600 × 10) + (10,800 × 16)	= 238,800

42 B

43 A

Sales contribution on actual sales	$50,000
Less: Adverse total variable costs variance	($3,500)
Actual contribution	$46,500

No adjustment is required for the favourable sales volume contribution variance, as it will have already been added to the budgeted contribution to arrive at the standard contribution from actual sales ($50,000) given in the question.

44 D

45 A

For the first 10 hours of calls only the fixed line rental is charged therefore the answer cannot be B or D, which show no costs until a number of hours have passed. Graph C shows a variable cost is charged from nil to a maximum number of hours which is incorrect.

46 B

144,000/630,000 × 100 = 22%

47 A

144,000 – (630,000 × 12%) = $68,400

48 B

Process account

	Units	$		Units	$
Materials	2,000	8,000	Normal loss	200	350
Conversion		4,500	Output	1,700	11,475
			Abnormal loss	100	675
	2,000	12,500		2,000	12,500

Average cost = ($12,500 − $350)/(2,000 − 200) = $6.75

49 D

Abnormal loss account

	Units	$		Units	$
Abnormal loss	100	675	Scrap	100	175
		675	P&L		500
	100	675		100	675

50 A

Idle time + General overtime = (15 hours × $12) + ((10 hours − 4 hours) × $6) = $216